The Litany of Loreto

The Rt Rev. Charles Renfrew,
Ph. L., S.T.L.
Titular Bishop of Abula

All booklets are published thanks to the
generous support of the members of the
Catholic Truth Society

CATHOLIC TRUTH SOCIETY

PUBLISHERS TO THE HOLY SEE

Contents

'The Litany of Loreto' is based on a series of articles by Bishop Renfrew which appeared during 1983 in the Scottish Catholic Observer. It was updated in 2012 by the CTS editorial staff.

Bishop Renfrew writes as follows:

When I started to work on Litany of Loreto I didn't know how much praying and reading and research would be involved.

As time went on, I began to enjoy more and more dipping into the theology of Mary, the Mother of God, and trying to translate this Mariology into reasonably understandable and devotional terms for the reader not only to learn from, but to enjoy a little too.

Above all, the writing has involved me, as I hope its reading will involve you, in a deeper appreciation of and love for Our Lady - and should it achieve this in even one reader, it will have been worth the whole task. Indeed, I may say, it has already been worthwhile for what it has achieved in me.

So, get out that prayer book at the Litany of Loreto and read it, pray it, with each invocation. Take out the hymnal too and re-read those lovely hymns to Our Lady which you have probably sung out in church without really plumbing the depths of their meaning. Take the rosary from your mantelpiece (or, better, your pocket) and ply the beads in honour of Jesus and Mary.

And the blessing of the Son of the Mother will certainly be on you!

✠ Charles Renfrew
Glasgow
Feast of Our Lady of Lourdes, 1985

Preface

I suppose there are as many forms of prayer as there are people. We all have our own way of talking to God. Some are gifted with a certain ease in contemplation - sitting quietly in the presence of God and letting him act on us, with very few words. Indeed, this openness to God's action upon us is something worth practising and striving for. Others find this more difficult, but stick to simple forms of vocal prayer learned when they were young. Indeed, St Thérèse of Lisieux always maintained that she could never get beyond the words 'Our Father' in the Lord's Prayer, so full did her mind become at the very word 'Father'.

Other people need pit-props in prayer - the Rosary, prayer books, the Thirty Days' prayer - and have their special 'favourites' amongst the prayers of the great saints.

The important thing is to pray - to get into contact, and raise your mind and heart to God frequently, wherever you may find yourself: it is a question of giving time to God instead of to other things. St Benedict's 'To work is to pray' must be interpreted correctly - he did not mean that work was a substitute for prayer, but that it is possible to raise your mind and thoughts to God even during work. His adage must not be used as an escape from contact with God, even during work.

Maybe a new definition of prayer (another to add to the thousands!) would be simply 'to live constantly in the presence of God.'

Never, but never, say 'I'm not very good at prayer'. If you do, my answer would be 'Then become good at it', for it takes the grace of God and practice of years to be constantly aware of the presence of God all around you in everything and everyone. Besides, you must not look always for consolation in prayer: sometimes it is the constant doing down of distractions which makes for the best effort, and it is effort which the Lord looks for, and not merely results. Surely one of the finest prayers of Our Lord himself was his agonising prayer in Gethsemane. And the answer to that particular prayer was a clear 'No' from the Father.

Nor must prayer be looked upon as a mere asking, pestering of God for favours. Prayer, like the Mass itself, can be the sheer adoration of God, thanking him for his innumerable benefits, confessing our own sins and unworthiness; I would say that these aims in prayer are the proper priorities, way ahead of asking for favours: if your prayer has become sheer adoration, there will never be a need for any other sort!

Mary, God's mother and mine, help me explore the treasures of this ancient prayer in your honour. Amen.

Litany of the Blessed Virgin Mary

Lord have mercy.
Lord have mercy.
Christ have mercy.
Christ have mercy.
Lord have mercy.
Lord have mercy.
Christ hear us.
Christ graciously hear us.
God the Father of heaven,
have mercy on us. (repeat)
God the Son, Redeemer
of the world,
God the Holy Spirit,
Holy Trinity, one God,
Holy Mary,
pray for us. (repeat)

Holy Mother of God,
Holy Virgin of virgins,
Mother of Christ,
Mother of divine grace,
Mother most pure,
Mother most chaste,
Mother inviolate,
Mother undefiled,
Mother most lovable,
Mother most admirable,
Mother of good counsel,
Mother of our Creator,
Mother of our Saviour,
Virgin most prudent,
Virgin most venerable,
Virgin most renowned,
Virgin most powerful,
Virgin most merciful,
Virgin most faithful,

Mirror of justice,
Seat of wisdom,
Cause of our joy,
Spiritual vessel,
Vessel of honour,
Singular vessel of devotion,
Mystical rose,
Tower of David,
Tower of ivory,

House of gold,
Ark of the covenant,
Gate of heaven,
Morning Star,
Health of the sick,
Refuge of sinners,
Comfort of the afflicted,
Help of Christians,

Queen of Angels,
Queen of Patriarchs,
Queen of Prophets,
Queen of Apostles
Queen of Martyrs,
Queen of Confessors,
Queen of Virgins,
Queen of all Saints,
Queen conceived
without original sin,
Queen assumed into
heaven,
Queen of the most
holy Rosary,
Queen of the Family,
Queen of Peace.

Grant, Lord God, that we, your servants,
may rejoice in unfailing health of mind and body,
and, through the glorious intercession of Blessed Mary
    ever-Virgin,
may we be set free from present sorrow
and come to enjoy eternal happiness.
Through Christ our Lord.

Looking at the Litany as a Whole

Antiphonal prayer is a very old type of prayer from the earliest days of Jewish worship. I suppose we best know it officially from the Responsorial Psalm - the reader or cantor reads or sings the psalm, and the congregation replies with the repetitive antiphon - with the same words and tune throughout. The same applies to a litany - the invocation is called out and the whole body of people reply with a simple, 'Have mercy on us', or 'Pray for us'. There are some very beautiful old litanies in the Church's treasury - the Litany of the Saints, the Litany of the Holy Name, The Litany of St Joseph, the Litany of the Precious Blood, the Litany of the Sacred Heart, etc.

In the Litany of Loreto, Our Lady's help is called for under no less than forty-nine titles, each expressive of one or other of Our Lady's virtues.

The first twenty titles indicate the dignity of the relationship between Mary and God and man. They show her excellence as the prototype, after her Son, of Christian perfection.

Then follow seventeen titles, many associated with the Old Testament prophecies of her power and office.

Finally, she is addressed twelve times as Queen - in terms which express the broad terms of her queenship. The litany ends with the prayer from the common Mass of Our Lady, seeking health of mind and body, and deliverance from present sorrow to future joy.

Before embarking on an individual analysis of the various titles - which will give us a deep insight into the virtue of Our Mother - could I ask you to have a copy near you and look at its broad outlines and divisions? This will give you a better idea, for a start, of the riches of the prayer which maybe you have said or answered in a merely routine fashion.

Indeed, to avoid this routineness, which is a danger in all well-known prayers, I think you have to study the prayer as a whole, and say it, above all, slowly: otherwise, its depths escape you, and you are faced with another precious gem before understanding the previous one.

Machine guns of praise

Look upon litanies as machine guns of praise, title following title, plea for mercy following plea for mercy. For do we not need the intercession and care of our Mother and of all the court of heaven to aid us through our particular Valley of Tears? We know from having used other prayers to Our Lady that she is clement, loving and sweet. We know that never was it known that anyone who fled to her protection was left unaided. We are sinful and sorrowful, standing humbly before her, but she, the Mother of the Word Incarnate, will not despise our petitions, but in her mercy will hear and answer our every prayer. For she is our Mother, and we her humble and weak children. Indeed, maybe the magic word 'Mother' is the key to it all, and the root of our devotion to her and our claim on her 'now and at the hour of our death.'

Why Loreto?

This litany in honour of Our Lady is called after the shrine, the Holy House of Loreto, where it was used among pilgrims from the mid-sixteenth century. The litany did not originate at Loreto, but is traceable to the early Middle Ages: it is greatly influenced by titles of Our Lady used in the Eastern Church. Indeed, the litany's earliest manuscript dates as far back as 1200. But its popularity spread through thousands hearing it at Loreto and taking it to various lands on their return home from pilgrimage.

In 1558 it was published as 'The Litany of Loreto' by St Peter Canisius at Diligen in Germany - and his is the oldest-known printed copy of it. Despite efforts to change its texts, Sixtus V granted his approval to the original form and recommended preachers to propagate its use. In time, new titles were introduced.

Pius VI added 'Queen of all Saints' on his return to Rome after his long captivity; Leo XIII added the titles 'Queen of the Most Holy Rosary', 'Queen conceived

without Original Sin' and 'Mother of Good Counsel';
Benedict XV during World War I added 'Queen of Peace';
Pius XII on the occasion of the definition of the dogma of
the Assumption added 'Queen Assumed into Heaven'.

The Invocations of the Blessed Trinity

We commence the litany, like so many other litanies, with eight invocations to Father, Son and Holy Spirit, the last of them summing up the others, 'Holy Trinity One God'.

Apart from being a lovely and fundamental devotional act in honour of the Trinity, these early invocations stress to us that all glory and honour goes to God - the One God in three Persons. No creature, even Our Lady, can usurp the fundamental place of honour due to God alone - so always in the first place in all our adoration and praise, goes praise to the most Blessed Triune God.

It is as though the Church is saying, 'Having established the proper priority of praise to God, then we can go on to praise him in his creatures.' In other words, we use Mary and the saints as intermediaries in our praise of God - in no way inhibiting his claim to top priority, for he alone is the creator. Our Lady and the saints are creatures.

On the other hand, to praise the creations of the master is surely to praise the master himself. If I admire a friend's house or garden or the works of art he has created, I am praising my friend indirectly. 'What a lovely garden! You must have put a lot of loving care into that!'

In the case of Our Blessed Lady, the fact that the second person of the Trinity became man, took on flesh, and used a chosen woman to be his Mother surely indicates that the Mother must be rather a special person, a special creature chosen from all women of all time to be the mother of God made man. Surely we can ask her, especially as she has been handed on to the whole human race as Mother and Queen, to bear our prayers to the throne of her Son in heaven. It is not idolatry to have her image in our homes and churches to remind us of her, worshipping God through her - not the woodwork or the plaster as though they were idols.

Mother, clothe my prayers suitably to present to your Son in heaven. Amen.

Holy Mary

The very word 'holy' comes from Anglo-Saxon meaning 'healthy'. What, after all, is health? Does it mean we go leaping about the place running marathons, or doing press-ups and toe-touches? Well, that is one rather minimal sense of the word. But many people who can be classified as 'sick' or 'unhealthy' certainly qualify as holy people, healthy in its fullest sense.

In my book, to be really healthy is a disposition of mind rather than of body. One must possess a sense of the proper priorities, a sense of balance, a sense of good and evil, a sense of judgement, a sense of one's own destiny, of one's talents, of the destiny and talents of other people.

And as the supernatural is founded on the natural in many ways, the holy person must have a sense of balance and judgement and priority and, above all, of his own place in the universe and his own destiny as a child of God.

Similarly, holiness does not depend on a sort of sickly look, barring one's eyes from the world round about - the sort of 'plaster saint' look common to baroque statues. There is nothing namby-pamby about holiness. Of course, prayer and detachment from the world come into the life of the holy person, but the crux of holiness is love of God and of fellow man. We must look up to see and contact God, but we must not be blinkered from the joys and sorrows in the life of our fellow men. Even the hermit saints themselves soon discovered that they became the centres of attraction, often finding themselves with a score of disciples willing to learn their trade! So we see that though the 'man of the world' finds holiness difficult, the 'man in the world', very much a part of history, is the real saint provided he constantly remembers who he is, who made him and where he is going. He gets on with living as a precious part of history and accepts the challenges all around him, raising everything to a sacramental value as coming from God and returning everything to him to whom all things belong.

Mary was holy in the first place precisely because she knew her place. 'For He that is mighty has done great things for me, Holy is His name ...' From her very first calling she showed a natural prudence and wonderment, but then she accepted herself as a woman in history, a history made by God, executed by man.

Moreover, God touches people and things and makes them holy - the priestly blessing, the consecrating words. God and his holy people are infectious. She was not merely touched by God, she bore him made flesh in her womb, spent thirty years with him, accepting the holiness which flowed from his every heartbeat. And so every fibre of her being was sanctified. Maybe some of his holiness will rub off on us through her!

Holy Mary, Mother of God, pray for us sinners, now and at the hour of our death. Amen.

Holy Mother of God

I remember a group of us discussing with an old parish priest of immense devotion to Our Lady which of her titles we should put in neon lighting above a new shrine.

We all had our suggestions, and the old priest remained silent until we had exhausted all of our ideas. Then he said, 'There is only one title of Our Lady which sums up all others, and that is going above the shrine - and the title is Mother of God!' He knew all the time, like so many old parish priests - but this time he had hit the jackpot: he was right.

For when you come to think of it, the fact that Mary was chosen from all women to be the Mother of God made man, tells the whole story. A woman chosen to be God's mother must be the very best in every way, full of grace and virtue, unspotted and unstained, untouched by the world around her, gentle and courteous, kind and loving - stop! We are almost finding a new litany within the litany!

This is why people do not really have trouble with understanding the dogma of the Immaculate Conception or the Assumption. Such a woman chosen to be Mother of God must surely be totally free from all sin. 'A woman will crush the head of the serpent' - she must have total mastery over the devil and evil from the first moment of her conception; she must be conceived free from all sin to house the Author of all Good.

Moreover, she must enjoy certain freedoms and privileges. She was not spared suffering for, like her Son, she had to play her part in the redemptive act of mankind - indeed, through our suffering, so has each one of us, sharing in the cross, 'making up what is wanting in the cross of Christ' as Paul so boldly says.

But that she be preserved from the corruption of death, which has traditionally been linked with evil and sin, and assumed body and soul into heaven, is a privilege which is logical and which cannot be denied her.

What admiration do we rightly have for true loyalty - people who give up their whole lives in the cause of their country, whose pains vastly outweigh any privileges they have! And how much admiration do we have for the mother of a king or queen, from whom so much graciousness stems. Here we have the Mother of the King – awesome thought. For who can be closer to the child than the mother?

Once we admit that Mary was the chosen Mother of God, then we are willingly forced into the realm of protection and privilege for her. What person, human and frail, could undertake the immense and almost impossible responsibility of harbouring and bringing up Jesus, unless shielded, protected and intensely loved by God - put in the very few words, the first description of Mary we have, and that from an angel, 'full of grace'. Of course the Lord was with her from the very start, of course he was with her for his whole life on earth. He is with her still, for is she not his Mother and his Queen?

Mother of Jesus, be our mother too and share God's grace with us. Amen.

Holy Virgin of Virgins

Virginity is a fundamental word when we come to think about or talk of Our Lady. The Church makes it clear that Mary was a virgin before, during and after the conception of her only Son, Jesus. 'What is in you is there from the Holy Spirit.' No man was in any way concerned with the birth of Jesus; no man approached the pure Virgin at any time afterwards. Jesus is the sole begotten Son of Mary. He had no siblings. When modern translations appear talking of the 'brothers and sisters of Jesus', they have translated a wide-ranging Hebrew idea which can mean anything from 'brother' to 'tenth cousin'. To give Jesus a brother or sister would be at once to deny the virginity of Mary. Joseph, as we have been taught from our earliest day, was only the guardian or foster-father of Jesus, in no way his true father, or else, again, we would be denying the virginity of Mary.

Because of her privileged position, unrivalled by any other human being, Mary had to be truly a virgin. Who could be the brother or sister of Jesus, Son of God, without encroaching into the Blessed Trinity? What man could approach the Virgin when her womb had been filled by the third person of the Trinity, the Holy Spirit? So many of the doctrines regarding Our Lady are highly logical, given the initial premise that she was chosen before all time to be the Virgin Mother of the Son of God. She had to be conceived immaculate, and she had to be before, during and after the birth, a virgin.

Some people consciously choose virginity in order undividedly to give their whole life to Christ and his gospel (eg, priests, and religious brothers and sisters). They fully recognise the nobility of marriage, for, after all, they were born through marriage themselves, and they teach, nurse and deal with the children of marriage. But they wish to liberate themselves wholly from the sacred obligations to husband, wife and family, in order to devote themselves entirely to God. In a sense, it would not be fair to wife or family if priests and religious brothers and sisters were to have to share obligations to them, and deep love of them, with their unstinted service of the Lord. This does not mean that they are free from love of their fellow men and women, but it becomes a controlled love. The priest, so beautifully called 'Father', renounces literal fatherhood in order to belong to all others on this earth and have his fatherly interest in them all - 'belonging to all families, belonging fully to none'.

The vow of celibacy taken by men and women is not meant to be a chain binding them and constantly nagging them, but a form of liberation to free them to follow more closely in the footsteps of Christ, and to give themselves entirely without distraction or divided love to Him. This vow does not make them unnatural or insensitive, like robots, but enables them to plunge totally into the love of the Lord, which they spread to others throughout their lives amongst the people.

Mary, ever Virgin, teach us all to be pure and unstained. Amen.

Mother of Christ

It is important to know the full significance of the name JESUS CHRIST. The word JESUS means SAVIOUR. The word CHRIST means ANOINTED. So, Our Lord is the anointed saviour of mankind.

Anointing was used all through the Old Testament to make of people kings, priests or prophets - and Christ is King, Priest and Prophet. True, he was literally anointed by none other than the great sinner, Mary Magdalene. But he had been anointed in the mind of his Father before time began, chosen to be a priest sacrificing himself as Victim, a prophet to show the people their true destiny, and a King over all men. 'Jesus of Nazareth King of the Jews': note how when Pilate was approached to change that legend above the cross to "HE SAID 'I AM JESUS OF NAZARETH, KING OF THE JEWS'", he refused to do so; 'What I have written, I have written.' This was in itself prophetic. It was as though Pilate was being used to proclaim to the world the Kingship of Jesus, and Pilate would not be moved to change this prophecy, which has been ringing through the years since Christ's death on the cross. Indeed, if more people recognised his kingship, the world would be a less godless place today.

So, Mary is the mother of Christ, king, priest and prophet - Mother of the Anointed One of God. In some way his kingship, priesthood and prophethood rubbed off on her. We sometimes forget that the mother has great influence on the child, but that the child, right from the time of conception in the womb, influences the mother too. Surely her holy burden affected her from the moment of the angel's announcement and the conception of the Son implanted in her womb by the Holy Spirit.

So she shares in his royal kingship and she is Queen not only of heaven, but of earth. She is our Queen and Mother - royal in every fibre of her being, powerful as intercessor before the throne of God, full of queenly dignity, courtesy, affection and love for all her people. But being our Mother as well as our Queen, her role is even more important.

She shared in his prophethood too, reading the signs of the times right from the moment when she turned to the steward at the Cana wedding and said, 'Whatever he tells you to do, do it ...' and this is her message for us now too. She looks sadly down on a world, much of which has forgotten her Son and his cross, and maybe weeps at this ingratitude and blindness. But she is ready to help with her royal prerogatives and Mother's heart.

She shares surely in his priesthood, in his sacrifice for us, for she was called upon not to be privileged, but to share more intimately than anyone in the sacrifice of the cross. The sword which pierced her heart right through her life plunged deepest as she beheld him on the cross and held him in her arms at its foot. Yes, she knows what real priesthood is. She suffered intensely with him. There is no limit to her compassion, and she will show the same redemptive compassion to us all, if we only ask for a mother's care.

Mary, royal, understanding and priestly, look down upon your subjects and children redeemed by your Son, and pity us. Amen.

Mother of Divine Grace

The word 'grace' was probably introduced into our lives from early on. 'Full of grace', 'sanctifying and actual grace', 'grace before and after meals', 'the grace of the sacrament', 'the grace of the moment' . . . The true meaning of the word perhaps baffled you, like me. As I came to study theology in depth, its meaning again almost escaped me - it meant so much that it seemed to mean so little - like the adjective 'nice'.

Of course, literally (and this is where grace before meals comes in) it means 'thanks'. But its theological meaning is so much more profound; after years of thought and teasing it out, I have come to the conclusion that the best explanation of the word is the presence of God within us - a deeper extension of the name Emmanuel, God with us.

For God has implanted somewhere within each one of us a little touch of the divine, a bit of himself - and thus to know God, we must see and recognise Him in other people, and in ourself first. It is what is of the most profound good in you - it is something there - it is God who has flooded into your soul at baptism and has taken possession of you, and through this little magnet draws you to himself

- good calling to good, deep to deep - the large magnetic attraction drawing this little object toward himself, where it belongs. His presence can be increased within you by the sacraments, and by prayer, almsgiving and good works. And it can be lost in sin, especially serious sin (hence the term mortal sin, God 'dying' within you, as it were). This grace, this presence, is never static; it grows or diminishes with each recurring second. It flowers or decays, like creation itself.

Grace, then, lost by Adam, was restored to us by Christ on the cross. His redemptive act opened again to mankind, through baptism, the floodgates of the divine presence within us - and the sacraments of his love are the largest of the keys to open us more and make more space in our lives for the presence of God, which can overtake us gradually throughout our lives.

Now maybe we understand better why Mary is the Mother of Divine Grace. For she was free from sin: she was invaded by the literal presence of God made man: hence the first title she was called, not by man, but by God through the angel, was 'Full of Grace'; full to the brim of the presence of God. Hence she is mistress of Grace, for she is the Mother of Divine Grace itself, through having implanted within her through the Spirit the sacred body of the incarnate Christ, Christ made man to shed grace on the world.

And surely, then, she can help through her intercession with her Son, to spread that grace and make it felt and forceful in the souls of people who follow his way and open themselves to the fountain of his grace. I suppose, eventually, another way to look on grace is sheer love; for is not God love itself, and is not the love of him within us impelling us to share that love with others and allow others to share it with us? This is surely the key to family life, love, and to the life of the great human family, the brotherhood of man based on the fatherhood and the love of God.

Mother of Divine Grace, intensify God's love within us through Your Son. Amen.

Mother Most Pure

In these so-called enlightened times, it seems unfashionable to talk about purity, or even much to use the word 'pure'. Often, I wonder whether modern men are some sort of supermen regarding temptation: for nowadays things which seemed impure and indecent in granny's day are considered matter-of-fact, routine information for adults and children alike. Is the sexy poster any less dangerous now than in days of old? Have man's basic instincts and susceptibility to temptation changed over the years? If anything, I would say, man has become softer and more easily tempted than in tougher days before.

Anyway, there is within us a basic instinct for purity - so much so that there is still an inborn shame which goes with any form of wrongly directed love, or abuse of sex. It is hard to remain pure in a world where love is associated with sex, and the use of sex is supposed to have become a right of all, married or unmarried; it becomes increasingly difficult to be so different as to fight like mad to remain pure in both body and mind.

The devil's approach to temptations against purity is quite obvious: he makes present men laugh at past restrictions. Modern man, he says, needs no such restraints as in puritanical days. And so sex symbols and promiscuity are paraded openly today as though the sinfulness of impurity was a thing of the past, and man has been liberated from the battle for purity because it is almost assumed that he has lost from the start.

Before our eyes, then, base morals are peddled in the guise of art: on walls, on TV screens, and even through the voice on spoken media. Newspapers openly peddle sexy pictures and articles because 'The people like it, and it sells the paper', and sadly into even the most vulnerable of homes sexy plays, papers, magazines, calendars and videotapes flood. Even where there are young people around, man's basic low instinct for sensual pleasure is pandered to. It all sells, therefore it is good.

I am sure a modern newspaper editor or producer, if he bothered to read these lines, would classify me at once as fifty or even a hundred years behind the times, and would cry out, 'These are enlightened days - all that restriction belongs to Victoria's era and before ...' I would contend that in many senses these are darkened, not enlightened, days, that sins of impurity are no less serious now than they ever were, and that real corruption is being accepted as today's normal standard. In other words, the devil is certainly winning without having to do much work to succeed!

Now more than ever is there need for a pure mother to save us from the impurity all around us, to lead us into standards of body and mind which conform to the gospel of her Son. Let us fly, then, to the Mother who knew no impurity, who was immaculate, and who has still a special power over that same devil whose head she crushed, as though forcing from the beast all stench of sin and impurity. How we all love a clean house! What of our own little domain, our own bodies and souls, despite the muck around us?

Mother Most Pure, cleanse each one of us and dispel the corruption of impurity with which a godless world will always tempt us. Amen.

Mother Most Chaste

If you look up the word 'chaste' in a dictionary, you will find the definition: 'abstaining from all wrongful use of sex'. Note that this would apply both within and outside of marriage.

People nowadays wonder what lies at the root of so much evil and declining moral standards in the world. The reason first and foremost is surely a basic one: that man has ceased to believe in God. Other reasons spring from this, such as turning wholly to material things for temporary pleasure - 'eat, drink and be merry, for tomorrow we die'. Note how little the name of God is mentioned (except in blasphemy). Note how few people are bold enough to mention his name, and discuss his being and power. Nowadays, even religious lessons and media debates take refuge in anecdote, and seldom face up to telling the people of God's existence and the destiny of man, his creature!

We must, then, start with the admission of a basic power, uncreated and infinite, from whom all power derives - a God who has created man, and therefore guides his world and rules his ways: God who holds out to man his only hope, hope of a more perfect life hereafter beyond the limited fettered life we all know so well.

From the existence, then, of this supreme power above all people and all nature, we move to admit that he must make basic rules for man's own order and organisation, to help us reach the port of rest - like the captain disciplining his ship and his crew in order to arrive at port safely. Those who deny God are often those who wish to rule themselves, for they aim to make themselves God, as Satan tried to before them.

Just as many people tend to be vigilant about their appetite for food - diets and slimming methods abound in order to 'fight the flab!' - so the other appetite must be kept under control, and chastity is the positive virtue exercised in this control. As with other virtues, it does not come naturally without restraint and effort, and we must pray for this positive virtue to grow within us. Again, the chaste Virgin Mother of Christ will be our intercessor, and will lead us gently towards the bravery necessary to control ourselves to be chaste dwellings of the Spirit.

Mother Most Chaste, build up within us the tower of strength called chastity. Amen.

Mother Inviolate

To violate a person, item or law means to abuse it in some
way, and to treat it with disdain or contempt. This singular
title for Our Lady indicates that she is so holy, pure and
unique that in no way must she be treated as of little
consequence, let alone insulted or abused.

It is strange, but perhaps understandable, that down
the centuries men have either had the greatest love and
admiration for Our Lady, or else she has evoked in them
the greatest hatred. I have met people who not only deny
the various privileges of Our Lady, but are quite frantic and
fanatical against her. Why these two extremes? Our Lord
himself said, 'He who is not for me is against me . . .' One
can hardly be lukewarm about the gospel, or about Christ:
one cannot accept halfheartedly news of such importance
to our destiny, affecting every moment of our lives.

In the case of Mary, the Virgin Mother of God, we
must remember her function. By bearing the child Jesus
and presenting him to the world, she was stamping hard
and sure on the head of the serpent. Surely apart from Our
Lord himself, she is the greatest of Satan's enemies, and so
whilst he hates those who love her, he instills the greatest
venom into those who do not love her, and their love turns
to hate. Imagine hating a mother!

It has become unfashionable, even in some Christian circles, to talk about the devil. In the minds of some, talk of good and bad angels seems to smack of superstition. This suits the devil admirably, for he finds plenty of allies and cooperators to do his work for him, whilst he slides into the background with a sneer. How he must hate Mary, for she is the exact antithesis of Satan: humility versus pride, meekness versus arrogance, obedience versus disobedience, resignation versus rebellion, purity versus impurity - and so the litany could proceed!

I have tried over the years to deal with these adversaries of Mary, pointing out that if they believe that Christ is truly man, then he had to have a mother, and she must be a rather special person, endowed with the summit of grace (the presence of God), and with ever so many virtues and privileges necessary to her unique position in the redemption. But even then the battle is hard, for they have steeled their hearts against a mother, and this takes a lot of work to undo. And so I have resorted to prayer: prayer to Our Lady for her adversaries, for she is so much more powerful than any arguments. Tenderly, I feel, she will lead them home, 'for never was it known that anyone who fled to thy protection, implored thy help or sought thine intercession, was left unaided ...' Mothers can achieve so much more in their gentle way than even the most logical arguments. So we place her adversaries in her hands, praying that soon they will have her as mother too.

Note how gentle and unassuming are the devotees of Mary. For she is inviolate and inviolable - so very gently powerful as Mother and Queen.

Mother Inviolate, show yourself to all men, for we are all your children. Amen.

Mother Undefiled

To defile something is to spoil, profane or sully it. This world is full of defilement, both literal and metaphorical. The most startling example of defilement in modern times is vandalism of every kind, the spoiling of things, a sort of mindless destruction for destruction's sake. It points to a fundamental lack of grace, of appreciation of God's creation, of respect for other people's property. It is real devil's work, for he is the arch-despoiler.

Standards can be defiled, language can be defiled, goodness, holiness and purity can be defiled, stained, ruined, despoiled. Character and reputations can be defiled: I suppose it is the constant battle of evil against good.

Above all, sin defiles. Sin is anti-God: sin is preferring creatures to God, often preferring ourselves and our will to his, our ways and our plans to his. It is a violation of goodness, a spoiling of best order, a sullying of its opposite, true virtue. The sin of our first parents defiled the human race, involving a supreme sacrifice to put it right again. Our own sins defile ourselves and others. From the beginning of creation, then, life has been, is and always will be a battle against evil and a struggle for good.

How can man contend with evil all around him? Must he give in to it all, resign his colours and give up the battle? If he were alone in the battle, then he could never contend with the opposing forces ranged against him. But he is NOT alone. Christ not only redeemed him on the cross, but promises all strength necessary for the battle against evil. He has promised that he will be with us always, that He will not desert us even in our sinfulness: He is the strength of the weak, and the more we lean on Him, the more secure and strong we will be. There is no way can we fight the battle alone.

Through the lives of saints who have gone successfully before us, we are both edified and given example, and these people intercede for us before the throne of God in heaven. And, of all the saints, Mary, Mother of God and of us, is surely our help against sin, evil and defilement. Pure and undefiled, she will look after us in our battle, keeping us unsullied and pure in the widest sense. Indeed, when we compare our own unworthiness with the dignity and utter purity of Mary, it causes us surely to blush and feel great shame (a salutary feeling) that we fall so far short of what God asks of us.

And so the Mother Undefiled awaits our pleas for help, and we must pray with faith and love that at least a little of her purity will reach us. Above all, we can approach her with confidence to implore her Son to be with us always to save us from the 'contamination of sin'. The weapons for our battle are all there through the blood of the Lord, and through the example of those who have, with him, won the fight.

Mother Undefiled, guard us against sin and wrong, until the battle is over and we come home. Amen.

Mother Most Lovable

You might remember this invocation as 'Mother Most Amiable'. Probably 'lovable' is a stronger word than 'amiable', going deeper than mere friendship. It would be a good exercise to tease over in your own mind what makes a person lovable, and for this you will need to use your own examples of people you really love, and ask the question WHY.

The first bond of love is, of course, in the bosom of our own families: there is an undefinable love pulsating through those whom God has placed closest to you - mother, father, brothers, sisters. It is not something you talk about very much; it is just assumed, blood being thicker than water.

Then come, maybe, those who are on the fringe of family: kind aunts, uncles and other relatives who appear from time to time in your life: again, they really have something of the same blood, coming from the same stock as ourselves.

Then come those outside the family who play some important part in our lives, be they teachers, priests, school friends or our childish heroes whom we love from afar and in whom we can see no wrong. Still we ask, what makes people really lovable to us?

Undoubtedly, their attitude to us, their understanding and compassion at the time we need them most, the trouble they take with us, what they put up with from us, their presence in times of joy or sadness. With some people we find an instant rapport, love meets love, understanding meets understanding, regardless of whether they share our opinions. We love to be in their company, or if they are more distant to read about them or learn more about what makes them tick.

Sometimes this love is fostered by nearness, sometimes by distance. But always, sympathy and compassion are involved. We seem to reach the root of the being we love; not just a mere compatibility, but a profound unity and communion which transcends faults, failings, disagreements and arguments. In fact, it is often said that where there is profound love there is no need for actual communication by words: we can walk or sit in silence with such souls amidst a mutual union and understanding that cannot and need not be put into words.

Some of the saints appeal to us; others do not. Maybe those with whom we find something in common make the deepest impression on us. But of all the various saints, and there are thousands of them, one person stands out as lovable and understanding, though we have never seen her. Those who have, like Saint Bernadette, could never really describe the love which flowed from her, the Mother of God. Her very presence was enough. But we have not seen her, and surely pictures and images fall so short. But it is not the external appearance which causes us to love someone: it is surely the presence of God within them which leaps out at us and brings to life his presence in us.

We love Mary for what she is, for what she was chosen to do, for how she did it, for the few things she said, and for her closeness to her Lord. What makes her truly lovable is her nearness to love Itself, her awesome close connection with the second person of the Trinity become man through her.

Mary Most Lovable, share your Son, love itself, with us. Amen.

Mother Most Admirable

'Mother of God and daughter of thy Son,
  yet mother mine,
The Lady of thy Lord, the Holy One, thy Child Divine,
Show me thy wondrous babe, O Mother Maid,
  foretold of yore,
The treasure on thy virgin bosom laid let me adore ...'

There must be good reason for us to admire something
or someone. We admire works of art, great monuments,
daring deeds of heroism and qualities in other people who
rise to great heights in the world. We admire people who
can do things impossible to us; those who sometimes lead
or teach us, or show us the real way to live. The greater the
magnetism of the personality, the greater the admiration
evoked in us.

Admiration is a form of wonder at God revealing
himself to us in creation or in creature. Our eyes open wide
at the beauty of the rose or plant, or at the wondrous gifts
with which a great person has been endowed by God. How
totally admirable is God!

What unspeakably admirable qualities Our Lord
exhibited - the great calm and patience, the constant
living in the world yet in the presence of the Father, the

admirable capacity for patience and for suffering, the restraint and simplicity.

What in Mary, his Mother, makes her most admirable? Surely the way she accepted prudently the overwhelming news that she was to become the mother of the Messiah; the compassion shown at her visitation of Elizabeth, and the beauty of the Magnificat. How we admire the circumstances of the birth of the King in a manger -the prudence in flying from Herod and the hidden life at Nazareth. What of the distressful moments when her son was lost in the temple? How she moved into the background during the public life of Our Lord, at the start of which she acted so admirably during the wedding at Cana. And then the journey to Calvary, the death of her son, the plunge of that sword promised to be with her all her life. How admirable her words and her deeds; her perfect fitting into the picture of the redemptive act on the cross. Not a foot wrong, not a word out of place.

In our own thoughts of Mary we meet with so many qualities worthy of our admiration. Both the Sacred Heart sisters and the Schoenstatt sisters have made this title their special prerogative, for admiration is a sign of honour and loyalty, and, above all, of love. And so we pray to the most admirable Virgin:

Mother of God, commend me to thy Son as here I bend,
And O, commend me when my task is done and life shall end:
within thy outstretched arms I leave my heart,
    Lady, with thee –
A worthless gift with which thou wilt not part eternally.
Amen.

Mother of Good Counsel

Mothers are good counsellors. I remember having to lead young boys along the first steps of deeper relationship to Christ by chatting to them – 'spiritual direction'. Always I started by asking, 'What does your mum think of you - your good and bad points, for she knows you better than anyone in this world, and would be your best spiritual director!' Of course, mothers know their children best, having watched them grow from babies, and having observed from the earliest days what kind of character their infant was developing into. And so, even in later life, mothers can guide their children, console and hearten them, and be their counsellors.

Therefore, Mary, our Mother, can do this for us in many ways, if we only ask her to play a part in our lives. For example, she teaches us by her own virtues. And surely first of all her virtues is her faith. As the Second Vatican Council pointed out in the lovely chapters on Our Lady at the end of the Decree on the Church (*Lumen Gentium*, CTS Do 726), Mary received Christ into her body, but also into her soul by her complete and utter faith. As Saint Elizabeth said: 'She believed that the promise made to her by the Lord would be fulfilled . . .'

Then would surely come her obedience. Again, as the council points out, 'The knot tied by the disobedience of Eve was untied by the obedience of Mary: what Eve bound up by her disbelief, Mary loosened by her faith.' And what of her purity, her simplicity, her humility and docility, the burning love implanted in her from the first moment of her conception, making her full of grace and preparing her for her unique part in the redemption of mankind?

Yes, she counsels us in practice by her virtues. She also teaches us by the very few words quoted in the gospels: 'Be it done unto me according to your will,' 'For he that is mighty has done great things for me, holy is his name', and at Cana perhaps the best of all advice, 'Whatever he asks you to do, do it!'

Not only was she given to mankind as a Mother from the cross, but she was present at the birth of the church at Pentecost, and thus has an intimate place in the bosom of the church, the Mystical Body of her Son.

And so, she not only loves each of us, but has an intense interest in all our joys and woes. Surely she is the model of both extreme joy and exhilaration, and at the same time the model sufferer, sharing Christ's cross and its redemptive powers, as does each of us. For we are all concerned not in our own salvation alone, but in the redemption of all our brothers and sisters under the Motherhood of Mary.

And so, as the saints throughout history have all recognised, Mary stands ready as Queen and Mother to help each of us individually. She has shown her love for the humble at Lourdes and Fatima, among other places, for she sees in the humble and docile a model of herself, kindred spirits who have understood as she understood that the way to heaven, the gate, is small and low, and that we must all stoop to be assured entry. No one will be left unaided by a mother, or refused advice and counsel by this tender and most understanding of all women.

Mother of Good Counsel, direct me to your Son. Amen.

Mother of Our Creator

In a sophisticated age, full of technology and scientific know-how and advances, to admit that something is a mystery is almost an admission of defeat, and proud modern man does not like that. But surely the progress made in science, medicine and the arts is also dependent on God - and involves a mystery. We might well ask ourselves, 'Why did God not give us the cure for TB earlier? If only replacement hip joints had been available in granny's time! Why were our grandparents denied inventions such as the television (although some might question this particular 'advance')?' Indeed, it is as though God reveals knowledge, and solves mysteries, bit by bit to man.

Of course, if you do not believe in God, or pay him mere lip service, then you will look on each new discovery as a tribute to man. Yet the word 'discovery' implies something that existed already, in darkness and secrecy, and that all man did was to shine a light on it at a particular time in history.

There is something beautiful about a mystery: maybe that is why children get such a thrill out of life, for new discoveries are made each day and wonderful new things revealed to them in the course of growing up. Indeed, to the man of faith, life is a continuous thrill, and revelations of God come each day in his life. Life would be very dull if everyone knew everything about everything! Thus, discovery is one of the thrills of life and we would not want to live without it.

The great mysteries of faith make man ponder and try to reach into the hidden life of God - a thrilling adventure in itself. Is it not quite legitimate for God, the creator of the universe, to reserve truths to himself and not necessarily share them with man? Indeed, man's capacity to understand them is so limited. To bow before His mystery, and he himself is a mystery, keeps man in his proper place as creature confronting Creator, and prevents him from becoming victim to that awful pride which was angels' and man's first sin.

And so God is mystery, the incarnation is a mystery, the Trinity is a mystery, and so on. The mystery that concerns us here is, of course, the paradox of God becoming man in the womb of a created virgin. Our faith is full of paradoxes. A virgin mother; a king born in a stable; God crucified; victory in seeming loss; water becoming wine; wine becoming blood. We bow with awe at the thought of a young virgin housing her creator made man. Christ is God, God is creator, therefore Mary, the mother of Christ, became mother of her Creator. I find it a lovely mystery, something no scientist or doctor of technology can ever unravel. He must bow before the infinite power

and mystery of His God. Mysteries level us all - brainy
and brainless! - saving us from inflation, pride, snobbery,
and their like.

*Mother of Our Creator, help me to admit mystery without
even wishing to understand it! Amen.*

Mother of Our Saviour

'You will conceive a Son and you will call his name Jesus. He will be great and will be called Son of the Most High. The Lord God will give him the throne of his ancestor David: he will rule over the house of Jacob forever and his reign will have no end.' (*Lk* 1:31; 33)

How did this young virgin react to this revelatory news? Her feelings must have been many and varied to say the least: thrill, apprehension, amazement, wonderment. But after her cautious enquiry as to how it would all come about came total faith, understanding, belief and a stressing of her availability and utter obedience: 'Behold the handmaid of the Lord; be it done unto me according to your word . . .' Really, the Annunciation scene between the angel Gabriel and Mary could occupy our thoughts and give us deep contemplation for a lifetime. Indeed, it is hard to get past the first chapter of Saint Luke's Gospel, for it is so rich and full of sheer mysterious history.

Recalling that the name Jesus means 'saviour', this again fills us with awe, and explains Saint Paul's lovely passage in which he tells us that at the name of Jesus every knee should bend. Why? Because in this one name is summed up the role of Jesus, Son of God, Second Person of the Trinity. Think of it: 'The Word was made flesh and dwelt among us ...' Have we taken these words too lightly and let them become almost a cliché without realising what they mean to us all? What reverence we should have for the Holy Name of Jesus. A whole litany has been formed about this little name. And how sad we feel when this name is used in vain. The very name is in itself a most beautiful prayer which should always, not just often, be on our lips to remind us of the great mystery of the incarnation and redemption. What thrilling moments, the most important in all history, are recorded in this first chapter of Luke, which we should read and re-read time and again until new lights appear from God as to the wonder of it all.

And so the virgin Mary became the mother of the Word made flesh, experiencing the life of a man amongst men. Is this alone not reason enough to honour and love Mary, and to accept her as our Mother too? In the simple fact of Mary being chosen as the Mother of Jesus is the root of all theology concerning her, and all honour people have given her through the almost two thousand years since she was triumphantly taken up, body and soul, into heaven. The Redeemer, the Saviour, God made man, had to have a mother to be a real man, and Mary was chosen to be that Mother; a breathtaking thought and one which makes our heads bow to her as well as to her Son. What makes the mystery all the greater is that she is and always remains a creature: she must be able to plumb the depths of the mystery of the life of the Trinity, but in no way is she, a mere creature, a part of this. She intercedes with her Son; she does not grant the grace. And the more of a creature Mary is, with her own ordinary life in Nazareth, the more wondrous is the mystery that a creature should be used in such a way by God. Let us praise, honour and love her for her unique part in our redemption.

Mary, Mother of Our Saviour, ask your Son to keep reminding us that he saved us and opened for us the gate to heaven. Amen.

Virgin Most Prudent

In the next section there follow six invocations to Our Lady under the title 'Virgin'. I have already pointed out the nobility of the virginity of Mary and its cardinal place in Marian theology.

Why has the church singled out the words 'most prudent' to head the list of Mary's virginal qualities? The answer is fairly obvious. When the angel Gabriel announced to her that she was to be the mother of Jesus, surely her instinctive reaction would be to say, 'I am the mother, but who is the father? How can this be, for I am a virgin?' A prudent question indeed. In answer, the angel tells her plainly that the Holy Spirit himself is the Father, a truth which is spelled out also to Joseph. Having assured herself, then, of the divine logic of the situation, she gives her wholehearted YES or *fiat*, 'Be it done unto me according to your word ...'

Prudence dictated her journey to Elizabeth and her Magnificat, as well as the necessary (if difficult) journey for the census to Bethlehem, the flight from Herod and eventual return to Nazareth. Prudence dictated the way Mary acted upon losing the twelve-year-old boy and finding him in the temple. Prudence was shown in her treatment of the embarrassed couple at the wedding in Cana. Prudence was exercised all through the public life of her Son, when she seemed always in the background, not complaining or wanting to be 'in on the act'. But she was there when most he needed her - on the way to the cross, and at its foot to receive his lifeless body into her arms where it belonged, as though he was hers in death as he had been in his infancy and childhood. And yet again, present at the birth of his church at Pentecost, Mary's prudence was again ratified and secured by the gifts of the Holy Spirit.

Yes, prudence, shared with that of dear Saint Joseph, was the hallmark of those chosen to look after thirty years of the life of Jesus.

After all, what is prudence if not based on simplicity, humility, calm that leads to unbiased judgement, and the sense of doing the right thing and saying the right thing at the right moment? One is not really born with prudence: it must be worked for through more basic virtues, such as Mary had. It is the fruit of other virtues rather than a virtue in itself.

So, if we wish to follow her in her prudence, we must work at humility, simplicity, docility and obedience to the voice of God guiding us. He cannot guide the proud soul who takes all decisions by and for himself. The door of the heart must be opened to receive counsel and advice: the ear must be attuned to the constant voice of God, the heart to his constant presence within us and in the world around us. Then will come prudence in word and action, and quietness, calm and even courtesy. There is a priority of virtues, one leading to another. We need to be schooled in the basics before we can look for practical outcomes such as prudence. And so we ask this Virgin Most Prudent:

Teach us the foundation virtues in order that they manifest themselves in our everyday lives. Amen.

Virgin Most Venerable

A person who is 'venerable' is not necessarily ancient, like an old monument or relic from the past! Certainly, it can have this meaning - someone or something worth honouring because of their great age and worthiness of respect - but generally, the word denotes a person with great character and qualities or reputation. A venerable person is to be honoured and respected, and is worthy of the greatest admiration. Some way or another it has come to denote great wisdom too - the wisdom which comes of age and experience - as with the Venerable Bede. The title 'venerable' is given to a holy person who is about to be beatified or canonized; the first step on the way is when the Church permits us to call them 'venerable' (eg, the Venerable Margaret Sinclair).

It is strange that honours and decorations have magnetic charm for men in the world. The Honours List is scrutinized at New Year; the buff envelope inviting a man to become this or that, or to accept this medal or honour, is awaited. Say what they may, many men are eager to receive this sort of acclaim before their fellows. I suppose this one-upmanship is a form of snobbery or an injection of esteem. Let the reader value honours of this kind as he or she wishes, but with the knowledge that, really, when you think the matter out, they amount to very little, and somehow steal on earth a little of the happiness stored up for us in heaven. Dives probably had a few civic honours; Lazarus had none, yet his was the greater everlasting honour in the end. Francis of Assisi was not in the habit of accepting diplomas, honorary doctorates or titles of honour, but he is in the high place in heaven which is for the simple and lowly. Matt Talbot was never honoured by the government of Ireland, but has been put forward for the greatest honours in the church.

Worthy of the greatest honour, worthy of our greatest respect after Our Lord himself, is the creature, the Virgin, the Mother Mary, first and foremost because she was chosen from all time to fulfil the awesome task of being the Mother of God made man. Does this choice in itself not make her most worthy, most venerable? Does her Immaculate Conception not make her worthy of our awe and respect? Every facet of her life - every word she spoke and deed she did - cries out for our veneration; not the veneration we give to God, but the deepest respect and esteem we can give to any created person. Her vocation, unique and awesome, was the most wonderful ever to be asked of any creature, and her response to that constant call of God was given with a right good will, total obedience and wholehearted enthusiasm.

Let us, then, venerate not the honours of this earth or those who gain them, but the highest honour of all, to be called the Mother of God. Mary is so very worthy of our veneration in the best possible sense. All down the ages she has been venerated. May we not fail to recognise her unbounded faith and virtues, and with children's hearts venerate her in this world until we bow before her in veneration as the Queen of Heaven.

Virgin Most Venerable, give me some share in the love of your Son. Amen.

Virgin Most Renowned

'Renown' is something more than 'fame'. It involves being famous, but means that a person's fame and deeds have rung down the ages of history as a great melody, and have been written into history as exciting news to be read and re-read by future generations until the end of time.

Honour and devotion to the Mother of God is no new thing in the Church. The third century saw the introduction of two great feasts - Christmas, and the Presentation of Our Lord in the Temple, known as Candlemas. The Council of Ephesus in 431 defended the Motherhood of Mary (*Theotokos*) and gave rise to great growth in devotion to this Mother. Churches were founded in Jerusalem, Bethlehem and Nazareth dedicated to the events of her life. In the sixth century arose the feast of Our Lady's birthday on September 8; the Entry into the Temple on November 21; the Annunciation on March 25; the Assumption on August 15. In the seventh century came the Conception of Anne, celebrated in Eastern Churches on December 8 and later to become the Immaculate Conception in the Latin Church - and so on. There is a mighty collection of writings of the early Fathers of the Church on Mary, from Basil the Great (died 379) through to George of Nicomedia (died 880).

The Decree on Ecumenism of the Second Vatican Council states: 'In this worship of the liturgy, Eastern Christians extol Mary, ever a virgin, with hymns of great beauty. It was, after all, the ecumenical Council at Ephesus that made the solemn proclamation of Mary as the most holy Mother of God, to secure for Christ an appropriate and true recognition as Son of God and Son of Man, as the scriptures show him ...." (3.15)

To take but one hymn from the sixth century as an example of all these writings on Mary in East and West: 'We the people of all nations proclaim you blessed, O Virgin Mother of God. He who surpasses all things, Christ our God, in you has deigned to dwell. Blessed are we who have you as our defence, for you intercede night and day for us. And so we hymn our praise to you proclaiming, "Hail full of grace, the Lord is with you!" ...'

Indeed, from writings of the fifth and sixth centuries comes one of the greatest hymns in Greek, and the origin of the Litany of Loreto: the Akathistos, which comprises twenty-four stanzas, one for each letter of the Greek alphabet. The first twelve stanzas are based on the infancy gospels: the other twelve are of strictly theological character, expounding the same major Marian themes in which we take delight in our own times.

Surely, she is renowned. Surely throughout the ages her name has been on the lips of saints and sinners, in ecumenical councils, in the liturgies of East and West, in

the later development of the Rosary, the Litany of Loreto
and other prayers, some of the finest written by St Bernard
of Clairvaux, St Thomas Aquinas and other great Fathers
of the Church. She is built into the earliest traditions of the
church. This is true renown!

*Let your praises, Mary, ring throughout our age and
forever. Amen.*

Virgin Most Powerful

In the language of the world, 'power' denotes great strength. A powerful nation is one capable of crushing other nations. A powerful man rules the roost precisely because of his power. We talk of a power station, a powerhouse, a power struggle.

But need the powerful man possess in himself all the strength he needs? Not necessarily; all he needs is access to power, to hold the strings that unleash power.

The connotation of power does not necessarily concern war or political gain. The power can be for people's good. Power can be used well, not just as a means to dominate, rule or oppress.

When we talk of Our Lady being powerful, we really mean that she has access to power itself, that by her motherhood of the Son of God, she of all people will be listened to in our cause. It does not mean that she is God, but that she is the most likely of all creatures to have access to the divine power for the good of her children.

This power is certainly for our good. Being a chosen mother, Mary is surely the most understanding and compassionate of people; she knows where power and strength are needed in particular cases, and through her genuine compassion and sympathy, she knows when and how to ask God to apply the requisite remedy or power to heal some particular sorrow or trial.

And so her power is a gentle, motherly power. In this way, power can be understood as a positive influence. Would to God we were wise enough to be influenced by Mary, caught in her gentle sway, affected and attracted by her sheer virtue and example, willing to imitate her in every aspect of her human, most human nature and life experience.

Like a magnet her power attracts us, her virtues attract us, her silence and reticence attract us. There is the sort of power which is the best of all; the power for good rather than evil, the use of power for sharing strength and resources, rather than for domineering and deprivation.

And so let us place ourselves under the gentle sway of the Virgin most Powerful, and we will be drawn into the range of her power and influence, and we shall feel safe and sheltered under her power - or, rather, the power shining out through her from God himself. 'For he that is mighty has done great things with me . . .' 'The power of the Holy Spirit shall come upon thee . . .'

Mary, Virgin All-Powerful, look with compassion on us who are weak. Amen.

Virgin Most Merciful

'Mother of Mercy' is a title we know well from prayers and hymns in honour of Our Lady. I wonder have we ever paused to think a little more deeply about the part played by Mary in the tender mercy of our God?

'Mercy!' is a plea constantly used in the church's prayers, and rightly too, for the act of redemption on the cross was an act of mercy. Mankind had sinned and was worthy of punishment, but God was merciful to us, as the father was merciful to the prodigal son despite his misdemeanours. 'For with him there is mercy and with him plentiful redemption ...' 'God of mercy and compassion ...' 'Have mercy on us, O Lord, have mercy!' 'Be merciful to me, O Lord, for I am a sinner!' 'Jesus, Son of God, have mercy!' Yes, this word 'mercy' appears everywhere in our petitions and pleas, for we realise that only mercy will bring us again into his favour after our sins and the sin of the world. The most merciful act in all the world was performed on the cross at Calvary, and the tenderest of mercy ever shown. How often we cry out during Mass, 'Have mercy on us.'

Naturally enough, when it comes to seeking mercy, we will use every means possible, and the most acceptable person, apart from God himself, is his Mother, whom we ask to plead for us before the throne of God. How much mercy she had in her heart, joined as that heart was to the heart of her Divine Son! Surely his boundless mercy flowed freely into the heart of his Mother, who shared with him in the bringing about of the most merciful act in all history, the salvation of fallen man through suffering and death on the cross.

And so, rightly, Mary is called Virgin Most Merciful. Mercy always implies first an element of fault, and second an element of forgiveness through love. Man had fallen, but was to rise again through the cross and resurrection of God made man. There was no need for God to forgive man in this way, but he decided to do so, and to effect that merciful forgiveness through becoming man and dying on the cross.

We speak of God in the psalms as being 'rich in mercy' and we speak of his plentiful redemption. In other words, enough mercy was shown in his redemptive act to cover original sin and the sins of every individual man. Mary, conceived without spot of sin, had not the same need of his mercy - or, rather, his mercy poured out on the cross had been anticipated in Mary's case to touch her at the moment of her conception. And thus she was joined to his mercy before any other creature. This share in his mercy makes her merciful *par excellence*.

And so we cry, 'Hail, Holy Queen, Mother of Mercy!' for God is not just merciful, he is mercy itself, and she is the Mother of God's Mercy.

Conscious, then, of our own sinfulness, we cry to her to intercede with her Son for us, sinners that we are, and to beg a share in his mercy.

Most Merciful Virgin, show thy children the mercy of thy Son. Amen.

Virgin Most Faithful

'Faithful' means full of faith. Mary, as we have seen, showed this fullness of faith in the immediate way she received the message from the angel, as pointed out by Elizabeth: 'Blessed are you for you have believed that the promise made to you by the Lord will be fulfilled ...' No doubts, just one plea for explanation of how it was all to come about through the power of the Spirit; from then on, a faithful pursuit of the promise and the task given her by God. Remembering all the time that faith is a gift from God freely given, we must see that God gave such a gift to Mary at the first moment of her conception, and that as the body of the Lord grew within her, so did that faith which ruled her every thought, word and action.

Mary showed that faith at Cana and throughout Jesus' public life, during which he was reviled, misunderstood and mistrusted. With faith she followed him along the path which to the unbeliever must have seemed a path of defeat - but she knew it to be a path of victory, and as she held his body in her motherly arms at the foot of the cross, she knew that though he was dead, there was victory somewhere - and it lay in the Resurrection, the Ascension, and in her own being taken up victorious and splendid to heaven. Hers was, then, a life of faith.

'Faithful' also implies trusting. The faithful servant will trust his master implicitly and will not brook disbelief or mistrust. So many people now seem to believe in God, but when it comes to putting that belief into action by trusting God, they are found wanting. We may believe in him and all that his church teaches, but do we put this teaching into practice in our lives? If we do, then we must trust that every moment of our lives is planned and meaningful, that every suffering is meant as a sharing in his suffering, that every tragedy is in some way a yielding to him with full trust whatever he asks and demands of us in our human condition, according to his plan for the world and for each creature in it.

'Faithful', then, implies a deep loyalty and a fullness of service, and in this too our Mother is an example to us all. She was the most loving, willing and loyal of all the servants of God. In every detail of her life, both those we know from scripture and those we can only imagine for ourselves, she was loyal and trusting in her Son, fulfilling in every detail the Lord's plan for her in the salvation of mankind. She was near him always, though in no way imposing herself on him or the work he was to do. She was always present, always near at hand, to be used or not to be used - nor did this service seem to stifle her own initiative or personality. For surely it is apparent through scripture that she had a mind of her own, as at Cana, or the finding in the temple. But this unique and individual personality was joined in an equally unique way to that of her Son and her God, and the two wills were fused, which is surely the hallmark of all loyalty, service and faithfulness.

Virgin Most Faithful, teach me full and trusting service of your Son. Amen.

Mirror of Justice

The world seeks justice and peace. Indeed, peace can come only when there is justice throughout the world, for injustice leads to rebellion, war and strife. And thus there will be a continual struggle in this world for true justice, the justice which is God. Justice is built on truth, true values and true worth, starting from the fundamental truth that man is a creature of a just God, that man has specific and inviolable rights as man, no matter what colour he is or where he lives. Man is fundamentally equal to all others in the eyes of God, whose fatherhood extends to all men, making them brothers as his children and co-heirs to his kingdom. We all have a right to obtain his promise of eternal life and to be aided in this noble venture through life by one another, and by aggregations of men, such as the state and civil authorities, all of which must strive together in aiding man to his fulfillment, and to the realisation through this earth and his work on it of the promise of God's eternal presence in heaven.

And so we talk of peace, justice and truth. Truth shone through the simplicity of Mary, God's mother. There was no deceit, no double-dealing, but rather a full realisation of exactly what place she held in the history of the world.

With her was no sham, no false ambition, no pushing to the front, no seeking to out-do others, or to rule or command. She knew the truth of her own calling, and this truth made her truly humble.

With her, true peace. No warfare or aggression, no protestations about her Son or how people should treat him. She lived at peace, first with him, then with herself, and thus with everyone whose life touched hers. She did not stand up for him when he was oppressed or unjustly treated, for she trusted that what he was doing was right. She did not thrust herself forward to protest to the soldiery on the way to the cross: she just met his gaze with hers, a gaze of acceptance, mystery and motherly love.

Thus, she is the mirror in which all justice is reflected, not least the Son of Justice, Our Lord, her Son. All justice is contained in God, who is justice personified, and the Son of God, who came to show justice to the world, and through justice to conquer injustice, and to contrast the injustice of the world with the true justice of his Father. Mary, like a mirror, reflects the qualities of her divine Son, not least of which is true justice. Along with him, she 'fought' in a peaceful way for the salvation of every creature under God with no reservations, no distinction of persons, just a distinction of qualities and gifts to be used, loaned as they are by God, in the service of God for the salvation of mankind. What true reflections of Jesus do we see in Mary, his Mother and his mirror. This justice spoke from the cross, 'It is consummated', as though to say, 'Father, I have done what you asked me to do - now mankind is saved, all mankind', and Mary at the foot of the cross heard and understood.

Mirror of Justice, help justice and peace to come to thy children. Amen.

Seat of Wisdom

We talk of universities as being 'seats of learning'. Maybe this comes from the professors' chairs, where wise men sit passing on their wisdom to students. They preside over wisdom, their chairs being like pulpits, with their words being available to great crowds of people. They preside, as it were, from their chairs, to pass on wisdom and make sure that nothing of the intellectual power of mankind is lost as it develops throughout the ages under the God of wisdom.

What is true wisdom? Philosophers throughout the ages have set their minds to define this. 'Initium sapientiae timor Domini' says the psalm ('The fear of the Lord is the beginning of wisdom'). To see God not just as wise, but as wisdom itself, is to understand the fount of all wisdom and learning. Have we not all met men who pretend to be wise and learned, and yet look to themselves or pure science as the beginning of wisdom, instead of to the God of wisdom? God made the world, God made men with all their would-be learning and wisdom, and the very development of knowledge throughout the ages is in itself a sign that all learning comes from God, who gradually reveals more as the world grows older.

True wisdom, then, is surely to understand what man is, where he has come from and where he is going. Not to understand the message and purpose of life itself is to be truly ignorant, no matter what heights the professor has reached in science or letters. Sometimes we must learn from the meek and humble, from the simplicity of children what true wisdom is - and children inevitably make wise remarks, patently true and devoid of sham - for sometimes the wrong type of 'education' can obscure rather than elucidate the purpose of creation and creature.

Mary knew wisdom. She carried Wisdom within her: she lived with Wisdom and watched Wisdom in action in herself and in the world of two thousand years ago. Could she fail to be inspired with this contact with all that is true and good in learning? Did not wisdom burning within her scorch her too? With what results? It made her see more and more clearly the meaning of life, the urgent need for redemption, the goodness of the world and its sinfulness too. It made her understand fundamental virtues such as love, gratitude, faithfulness, trust, hope, purity and devotion, among others. Mary was steeped in virtue and wisdom, and thus we rightly claim her as the very seat of wisdom of all creatures.

She hosted wisdom, she learned at his feet and through his suffering, for gaining wisdom is painful; life itself is meant to be problematic and hard. But she saw the way through it all - and thus she was wise beyond words, and we must invoke her in our bold and painful efforts to educate the creature to the love of the Creator!

Show us, Mary, the true wisdom who found his home in thee! Amen.

Cause of Our Joy

Those who are constantly aware of the presence of God slowly but surely become possessed by his life within them, and are therefore joyful and optimistic. The source of all joy surely 'infects' the soul constantly in touch with God, and even the sadness of life becomes a joyful acceptance of God's will, and thus a source of deep-rooted joy.

In her unique contact and closeness to God, Mary must have shared this immense happiness, and must have radiated it throughout her life. She remains full of joy in heaven and will, of course, cause us to experience joy in our lives on earth. Think for a moment of the mysteries in her life which we call 'joyful'.

Reflect on the joy of the Visitation - the joy of fulfilment of a promise, the simple joy of anticipation, far deeper than mere earthly happiness or thrill at momentary passing happiness.

With joy in her heart she travelled to see her cousin Elizabeth, herself full of joy at the unexpected birth of a son in late life. What a joyful encounter that was between these two specially chosen people and the children in their wombs! Faith adds to joy, and faith vibrated in the words and thoughts which burst out into beautiful prayer at this holy and happy encounter.

And was there not supreme joy in the Bethlehem stable when the Saviour lay in the manger - there indeed a joy which reached into heaven and caused the angels to loose a cry of joy, which we repeat so very often in our own worship of the Redeemer. Christmas is all joy and happiness in its deepest significance even today, a temporary refuge from the sadness of life almost to another world, not of tinsel, trees and gifts, but, deeper, of a transport to heaven on earth, as we recall that God is with us and that he came in the silence of that starry and joyful night, still and calm and full of peace.

And what joy for the mother and foster father to present the child in the temple, and to hear the words of Simeon - although they promised a sword for the Mother, a sword which she must have known and expected, they ratified the promise of the Lord from outside - 'a light to enlighten the gentiles'. Having experienced this deep joy, Simeon could die in peace.

And last, a human joy, the joy of relief, at finding the child in the temple, attending to the business of his Father. The joy of renewed discovery, of relief from blame, the joy of realising that the Son of God was at work for his Father as a preface to the great act of service on the cross.

Joyful mysteries indeed! For she bore the source of all joy, and still stands joyful and happy, ready to pass on this intense happiness to her children. We are children of a joyful mother.

Cause of Our Joy, spread that deep happiness in all our hearts as we approach the supreme happiness of his presence in heaven. Amen.

Spiritual Vessel

There follow three titles of Our Lady under the general term of 'vessel'. Vessel means something which contains - be it a vessel for water or wine, a vessel for food or for precious things - it may be a sort of 'strong room' - or it can a container of goods and passengers (eg, to carry them across the sea). Mary was, of course, the vessel, the womb, in which was carried the Son of God. Pervaded as she was from the first moment of her conception by the Spirit, she has always been looked upon and invoked by the church as a spiritual vessel, full of grace and the presence of God.

Proclus of Constantinople, in the fifth century, had many things to say in honour of Mary which illustrate her sheer holiness as woman and mother, and her utter closeness to God. He called her, 'The paradise of the second Adam ... the place of union of nature, human and divine . . . the unique bridge between God and mankind.'

Proclus has a very beautiful metaphor connected with weaving:

'The great and marvellous loom of the Incarnation
on which was ineffably woven
the tunic of union,
in which the Holy Spirit was the weaver,

virtue the spinner, foretold from on high,
woof the ancient fleece of Adam,
weft the immaculate flesh of the Virgin,
shuttle the immense grace of the one whom she assumed,
craftsman in the end, the Word which entered into her
to hear what she ascribed to the Word.'

Mary, the only one who has lightened the pain of Eve, the only one who bore the redemption of the world, the only one to whom was entrusted the treasure of the precious pearl, the only one who begot Emmanuel in the way he chose.

'The only one'. Indeed, this was a unique vessel, a spotless vessel, a safe vessel on the journey of his life and ours. Mary carried him and she will carry us, her children too, through the tempests of life to the safe haven forever with God.

Safe, chaste and holy Vessel, bear me to thy Son. Amen.

Vessel of Honour

We call Mary the vessel of honour, not only because she housed all that is honourable, Honour himself, but because she herself, because of her mission in life and her preparation for that mission, is all that is honourable, is a seat of honour, and is due the honour of the people - an honour which is another expression of tender love.

Honourable women rose up in the course of history related in the Old Testament; women honourable for their own deeds, but each of them a pre-figure of the most honourable of women who was to come, Mary, the Mother of God, foretold from the garden of Eden.

Think of the long line of honourable women. Look into their lives and see that they all reflect one or other of the qualities which God had seen in Mary. *Eve* was born spotless too until she sinned, and the serpent who deluded her was to have his head crushed by the heel of Mary. Think of *Sarah* who miraculously became the mother of Isaac, the father of an innumerable people. Or of *Rebecca,* 'an exceedingly comely maid' destined for the son of Abraham, as Mary was destined in her own way for the Son of God. *Rachael* by her charms won the heart of Jacob; Mary, by her grace, won the heart of God. *Mary,* sister of

Moses, had her part to play in winning liberty for the Sons of Israel, whilst Mary, the Mother of God, has her part to play in mankind's salvation. *Deborah* the prophetess and *Jahel* the strong woman put an end to the triumph of an enemy 'until a mother arose in Israel' - Mary put an end to the triumph of the devil. *Ruth* found favour before Booz whilst proclaiming herself his servant - as did Mary, the handmaid of her Lord. *Abigail* turned aside the anger of David by her prudent humility; Mary obtains mercy for us sinners. *Judith,* by her bravery, saved her people; Mary, by crushing the head of the serpent, had her share in the saving of us all. *Esther* was of lowly birth, but won the favour of her king and became his spouse, as Mary won the heart of her Lord and shares with him the empire of the world. Esther was also exempted from the law which bound everyone else, as Mary was exempted from the law of sin. Finally, the *Mother of the Maccabees* was present at the martyrdom of her sons and offered them willingly to God, as Mary at the foot of the cross offered her Son as victim to the Most High.

Mary's honour lies in the fact that she was prefigured in all these honourable people: the world awaited her for so long and at last, at the Annunciation, she was revealed as the chosen one. Her honour grew as her Son began his saving mission, which culminated on the cross, with his mother nearby.

Honourable indeed Mary was, and honour supreme is she due because of being chosen of all women as the Mother of God, and because of the inevitable consequences of that choice. Throughout the ages she has been shown honour and will be until the end of time. 'Give honour where honour is due' we are told, and if ever honour were due, it is due to this most honourable of all women. Honour, not as God, but as the closest of all people to God.

Honour to you, O Virgin Mother, honour on earth and honour in heaven. Amen.

Singular Vessel of Devotion

What exactly is 'devotion? To be devoted to a person is to put yourself entirely at someone's service. We meet people who are totally devoted to their ageing parents or handicapped child. We meet people who have great devotion to the practice of the nine Fridays, or to the Blessed Sacrament, or to Our Lady. It means that they have a particular love of this person or practice, and spend a lot of time on it as opposed to other things. But always it includes the idea of service, 'devoted service', standing at the ready like a servant in time of battle, ready to be of any service whatsoever asked for by his master.

Thus devotion and devotedness imply humility (taking on the form of a slave), and obedience. Now surely Mary of all people was devoted to her son. She was his mother, but also his handmaid; obedient, always ready, always near, humble and submissive, ready to be in the forefront or background as required. Full, then, is she of devotion, a vessel of devotion overflowing and exemplary in service. What greater service has ever been asked of a person than was asked of Mary? She is for us the model of service, the model of the obedient and faithful servant waiting for the slightest command from her Lord - eager and willing at any cost to herself to obey, and fuse her will with that of the Lord, her Son but her Lord.

The word 'singular' is interesting. It implies uniqueness - 'only one'-ness. There was only one woman chosen from all time to be the Mother of God. Her uniqueness comes through all the prophecies of old about her. Mary was held out in the garden of Eden as the sole hope of the future, the antidote to the poison of the serpent (Genesis 3:15). 'In the head of the book it is written of me' (Hebrews 10:7). From all time she was awaited. David cries out, '... all the glory of the king's daughter is within!' (Ps 44. 11 sqq). She is the chaste spouse in the Canticle of Solomon: 'As the lily among thorns, so is my love among the daughters . . . Thou art all fair, O my love, and there is not a spot in thee ... Who is she that cometh forth as the morning rising, fair as the moon, bright as the sun, terrible as an army set in array?' (Cant 2, 2/4, 7/6, 10).

Isaiah singles her out as the great and singular sign of mercy: 'The Lord himself shall give you a sign. Behold, a virgin shall conceive and bear a son, and his name will be called Emmanuel ... a flower shall rise up out of the root of Jesse ...' (Is 7.14: 11, 1.) And Jeremiah - 'The Lord hath created a new thing upon the earth, a woman shall compass a man.' (Jer 31, 22).

All through the ages of the Old Testament Mary was prefigured and prophesied. She was singled out as something new in the way of creation; individual, singular, unique, and extraordinarily special. Young Mary herself must have been brought up in this very tradition, until the moment it all came true at the greeting of the angel - and then her true devotion commenced, never to end.

Devoted Virgin, lead me into complete service of your Son. Amen.

Mystical Rose

We must remember that devotion to Mary, the Mother of God, has been strong since the earliest days of the church: indeed, some of the loveliest prayers and poems in her honour are very old. Great and holy men exercised their minds on her various qualities from the earliest centuries - as in this poem of Theodotus of Ancyra in the fifth century:

'Hail, our such longed-for joy!
Hail, O name so full of fragrance!
Hail, O rapture of the church!
Hail, O memorial full of reverence!
Hail, O spiritual and salutory fleece!
Hail, O bright mother of dawning light!
Hail, O gushing fount of living water!
Hail, new mother and moulder of the new-born One!
Hail, O alabaster vase of holy ointment!
Hail, O humble space which welcomed to itself Him whom the world cannot contain!'

Or from even earlier, from Hesychius of Jerusalem:

'Mother of light, star of life.
Some call her throne of God,
others, great temple of heaven.
Yet others, virgin and fertile garden,
vine of fine grapes, flourished and untouched –

jewel-case whose gems shine more brightly than the sun,
quarry from which has been hewn without cutting
the stone which shelters all the earth:
vessel without steersman, charge of special things,
treasure which grows rich . . .
ark more spacious, longer, more noble than that of Noah.'

When we speak of her as a flower, flower of her race, we surely turn to that most beautiful of all flowers, the rose, perfect in shape, various in colour, beautiful in scent and form, protected by a thorn. For always in her life, despite her own dignity and that of the office given her, was the shadow of the cross, the threat of the sword piercing the heart, the thorn. If one thorn were missing from the crown of Our Lord, it was surely applied to the heart of his Mother, as she shared with him her sorrows and grief, not only at the death of her Son, but at the ingratitude of so many who spurn his blood.

A rose, then, blooming and ever adorning the universe, but always indicating that true love, true following of her Son must inevitably involve a thorn, a cross - daily. 'He who wishes to save his life must lose it.' Hail, then, the rose full of mystery - a flower, real but mystical, shrouded in deep and incommunicable mystery - yet available to you and to me through prayer and contemplation.

Rose of Mystery, let us not only see your beauty, but share your thorn! Amen.

Tower of David

Towers were built from the earliest days, and we find them frequently in the Old Testament. They can be the rather flimsy little towers built in the middle of vineyards to look out for wild beasts or thieves. Or they can be the central citadels of cities, to watch out for enemies or be the last bastion of defence.

People felt safer when there was a tower about, when they could be warned of oncoming doom, and the watchman on the tower was an important defender of the city against the enemy.

And so even in our own times, towers are the signs of both safety and prestige. How many architects have understood this and have incorporated towers into churches, let alone castles! The tower on the church is a sign of the safety of God's protection against all that is evil.

David's tower with its thousand bucklers stood as a powerful defence in Israel. No enemy could approach unnoticed: it was the guard against oppression, evil and the incursion of the foe.

This idea of defence, safety and security has been applied from earliest days to Our Lady. For as well as safety under the mantle of a mother, we must realise that the Mother is strong and the great defender against the devil. With Mary as our tower, our own cities of ourselves and the church will be defended and watched over constantly.

For there was nothing weak about this chosen Virgin Mother. Was she not for thirty years the defender of the God made Man? And will she not defend her children as she knows best, against temptation and sin?

I often think that instead of trying to right so many wrongs, and instead of teaching young people all about the temptations around them, we should positively encourage them to appreciate and love their tender Mother, and let her do the advising and counselling! To study the positive virtues of the Virgin Mary is surely in itself not only an antidote to evil, but a positive and strong instrument which will be near them in their struggle against what is evil. We do not have the answers ourselves, but there is so much we must leave in the hands of God and implore his help through the Virgin Mary who stands ready to help her children.

And so we apply to her, the tower of all strength, to do the fighting on our behalf, rather than face the battle alone with our own puny resources. Strong and noble tower of David, she will defend the church and her children against one she has already conquered. She will join her real strength to our weakness as any mother would lend her strength to the powerlessness of the infant, and thus make it strong.

Tower of David, tower of strength, defend the church. Amen.

Tower of Ivory

From as early as the fifteenth century BC we find ivory
from Egypt, Assyria and Africa used for ornamentation,
for boxes and statuettes and even the decks of ships.
Considered a precious material, it is used in the Song
of Songs of Solomon to describe the complexion of the
beloved, and the beloved is actually called 'Tower of
Ivory' in the same song (7:4). Hence it would indicate a
tower, not just for defence and watching, but something
beautifully constructed and precious and pleasing to the
eye - enduring and unchangeable, the fruit of much work
and craftsmanship.

And thus the title is given to Mary, the Mother of God -
for is she not specially fashioned, precious and endurable
and lasting? Sacred writers and theologians have exercised
their minds from early days on the theology of Mary, and
on her various qualities springing from the fact that she is
the 'Theotokos'- the Mother of God.

Basil of Seleucia (fifth century) cries out, 'O Most Holy
Virgin, he who gives you venerable and glorious titles does
not fail to tell the truth: on the contrary, it falls short of
your worthiness . . .' This precious tower of rare material
has caused scholars to vie with one another to bring out
more and more aspects of her gifts.

St Augustine (fifth century) writes so very beautifully:

'Christ is born:
God from the Father,
man from the mother.
From the immortality of the Father,
from the virginity of the mother;
from the Father without a mother,
from the mother without a father:
from the Father beyond time,
from the mother without seed;
from the Father as the beginning of life,
from the mother to put an end to death.
We still cannot contemplate
the offspring of the Father
before the morning star;
we celebrate his virgin birth in the dead of night ...
And he asks a question:
Who are you that with such faith have conceived
and soon are to become a mother?
The One who created you will be born in you.
Whence came to you such great goodness?
You are a virgin, you are holy.
Much it is that you have merited,
or better, much it is that you have received!
And she replies: 'Believe in him in whom I have believed.

Tower of Ivory, precious gift from God, watch over me and mine. Amen.

House Of Gold

I suppose the word 'house' is used so very often that we take it completely for granted. It denotes a shelter, a place where we are shielded from wind and rain and sun, a meeting place, an eating and sleeping place, a place of warmth and love. We hurry there when we are wearied or worried; we stay there to be nourished and to rest. It is a family place. Indeed, it gives its very name to the family 'The house of David'.

So important a part of our lives is the house that it forms many of the happy memories of days gone by, through association of the house with people who lived and died in it. Houses can be made of wood or brick or stone, but always there is the idea of safety and home.

Mary can be considered as a house in the sense that she housed her Son, she gave him shelter and safety and love. And as we are her children, we too can find shelter and safety with her, and true home and love. Her womb housed the one who embraces the whole world; thus we are in a special way joined with our mother and his. She can give nourishment and warmth to us, just as she gave it to her Son. In her we can find rest and peace from the storms around us.

And if we look for material to imagine what the house of Mary is made of, we cannot go further or better than the most precious of all materials, pure gold. For she is lasting and unchanging and rich and the most beautiful of all - thus she must be the house of the purest and most valuable of all gold, mined in the mind of God before all time, taken out from the roots of the people, refined and made precious even before she was born.

She gleams and sparkles in a dimly-lit world, giving light and hope to her children - a haven to run to, a mantle under which to take shelter.

Above all, with her there is safety and security. The golden house cannot be penetrated by thieves or destroyers. Hers is indeed a house of safety - standing out different and pure and infinitely rich amongst the poor dwellings of our souls.

Paulinus of Nola (fourth century) puts it very well:

'God created the holy maidservant
like the interior courtyard of a temple,
respectfully surrounded by reverence,
even to the rain and the dew.
Then he himself descended from the clouds of heaven,
on silent wing, soft and humble,
as once the dew fell upon Gideon's fleece.
But no one has succeeded
in penetrating the mystery, fulfilled

in the silent way
of God, become man in the womb of a virgin . . .'

House Of Gold, be a protection for your needy children.
Amen.

Ark of the Covenant

The Ark of the Covenant in the Old Testament was, of course, the miniature temple carried by the Israelites on their journey through the desert. It contained the two tablets of the law. When it was amongst them, victory came for the Israelites, and any who tried to capture it or bear it away met with disaster and were forced to send it back. It was finally enshrined in the temple of Solomon - and whether or not it was destroyed when the temple was burned, it vanished from the history of the Jews.

It was the symbol of the presence of God amongst his people. It was also the sign of the treaty, the covenant between God and his people. 'I shall be your God and you shall be my people.' Thus, it was totally holy and only the priests could handle it or enter into the holiest part of the temple in which the ark stood.

A symbol of this ark was, of course, the ark of Noah, a place of safety and refuge in the storms of the sea, a place itself of salvation of the people and continuance of the human race. The church is often called the ark of salvation, carrying its people over the storm-tossed sea to the haven of rest in life eternal.

Obviously, this can be applied as a title of Our Lady too. She was the ark which contained God himself as he grew within her. Thus she bore within her the salvation and saviour of the world. Hence her utter holiness and her immense part in the salvation of mankind. She was the bridge between the divine nature and the human - and with her is security and safe passage through the temptations of life.

Eleutherius (fifth century) writes:

'O Virgin, give us not only food for the body,
but also the bread of angels come down into your
virginal womb.
Make us fear the Son of God,
for he who fears God will keep his commandments
and purify his senses,
so as to gaze on the splendour of divine light.
After we have been granted purification of the senses,
there will follow enlightenment of the heart.
Hear us, then, O Virgin benign,
and receive our prayers.
O Virgin, pray to God for us that he will grant us
    perseverance,
and the strength to endure,
that peace may be strengthened and love increased:
so that when the day comes of sorrow and misery,
of calamity and sadness,

you will deign to present us to your only Son,
Who alone is God.'

*Ark of the Covenant, shelter us and bear us through life to
a safe port. Amen.*

Gate of Heaven

The infant class was busily engaged in drawing their ideal picture of heaven. Most of the drawings contained gorgeous pearly gates, high and noble, leading to beautiful gardens where people lolled about in eternal 'rest'. All, that is, but one small girl's drawing. It depicted the gates as very low and near the ground, almost impossibly low: one would need to be very tiny, humble and lowly before there was any chance of entering heaven. Yes, I would think that the gates of heaven are almost tiny: you have to become very humble indeed before there's much chance of getting in!

'Felix caeli porta' - 'Happy gate of heaven' is a title often given to Our Blessed Lady. The tinier one becomes, the more humble, the less there is of self and the more of God. Mary was indeed happy in her humility, she was glad to be humble, for in being humble she had shaken off all that was of self and left room, plenty of room, to be invaded by her God. Humility is a very basic virtue, for unless we have done away with all that is of self, thrown off all our inhibitions and false pretences, then we cannot expect God to enter the very depths of our beings. 'I live now, not I, but Christ lives in me, so said St Paul, after having exclaimed, 'I die a little daily ... With Christ I am nailed to the cross'. So the humble virgin whose will was fused with the will of her Son and her God teaches us the way in to heaven, and the way is a lowly way, a humble way - a tiny door.

Furthermore, Mary is the gate of heaven in so far as she is the most excellent of all teachers of the skill of reading the map to heaven. She knows her son better than anyone, she knows what he likes and what he wants. He is the way, she understands him and thus understands the way. Learn from her, just as we learn from him who is meek and humble of heart. What a signpost she is - not only passive, but active in our salvation in which she played such a part. He used her, as it were, as the gateway to life: we must use her as the gateway to life eternal.

We must strive, then, to be good pupils of so fine a teacher. First through imitation (with her help), of her superb humility. Then we must learn in our humility to carry him as she did - to be near to him always, and to fuse his will with ours. So many other things she must teach us too - to be calm and unruffled, to be prudent and yet most simple, to be strong and yet never aggressive, to be trusting and full of faith and hope and deep love, to be unobtrusive yet still to play our part as God wishes us to do in the history of the world in which we live and move and have our being.

Yes, Gate of Heaven indeed. But like her own way to heaven, it will not always be easy or comfortable: her word was a precious part of her being taught and teaching - for it was a sharing in his cross.

Happy Gate of Heaven, be my teacher and my guide and my way to heaven. Amen.

Morning Star

Stars are fascinating. They have absorbed people, young and old, for centuries, and have filled generations with wonder, joy and mystery. They represent the height of ambition - 'through difficulties to the stars'. Created by God, they praise him constantly. The righteous shine like stars, the wicked are like stars which have wandered off course. And the Morning Star is awarded to the righteous man (Rev 2, 28).

For the Morning Star is something special, or, in the case of this title of Our Lady, someone very special, shining and visible all the time, indicating God's glory, pinpointing the well-lit road to the throne of God like a bright signpost. 'Show me thy wondrous Babe, O Mother Maid, foretold of yore, The treasure on thy Virgin bosom laid, let me adore'. She is the great signpost, the luminous indicator to her Son. For she knows him, she understands him - and she will teach us all about him and lead us to deep and lasting understanding of God made man.

We must learn from others about Jesus, for we ourselves have not seen him. The gospels tell us about him and we revel in stories about what he did and said, and the wonders he worked. But who can show us and tell us more about him than his own Mother? Obviously, she was closer to him than anyone ever was, is, or will be.

Like a star revealing the glory of the heavens around it, so she reveals the glory of the King of Heaven within her and then in her home. O that we had the eyes to see him, the ears to appreciate his message, the sense to follow his way. If we find it all too hard and mysterious, for he is God and we are his creatures, then we must turn to a creature who was his mother and still is. She can lead us to knowledge of him which will be accurate and true.

How proudly a mother shows off her child to relatives and friends! There is nothing more attractive than a baby in a pram being shown off by a mother. And it is equally lovely to see a mother's pride in her son, even though the son is now a full-grown man himself. And how much pleasure it must give this Mother to be able to reveal her Son to those who wish to know him better. It is not just a question of knowing, it goes much further - it is a question of loving, a sharing by the Mother of the love of her Son - for who can love better than a mother?

And so we ask this glowing star, constantly visible to her children, to shine on us and reflect the glory of her divine Son that we may know him better, and knowing him better, love him more dearly.

Star of the Morning, show us your Son and lead us to his love. Amen.

Health of the Sick

What is it to be sick? Is it just to have a bad heart or liver or stomach, or to have a weak limb or a sore head? No, it can be much more than that. For many a person goes about very well in body, but sick in mind and in heart, and even sick with sin. There are as many types of sickness as there are types of people - and some sickness seems worse than others, but is not.

And so do we not all need healing for some kind of sickness? And we must turn to the God who made us, who knows our weaknesses and exactly where the healing is required. We must throw ourselves on his mercy and ask for deep and inner healing as well as outward healing. Had he not the greatest of compassion for the sick, the lame, the blind, the deaf and dumb - and, above all, the sinner? 'Which is easier to say, "Thy sins are forgiven thee," or "Rise, take up thy bed and walk? "' And to show that he had power over all sickness and sin, he cured that paralysed man, curing his sins as well as his paralysis.

And so we can assume that Mary, his Mother, is equally touched by the sins and miseries of men. She herself was well acquainted with sorrow and suffering. She saw his concern for the sick and the oppressed, and she saw him sick and oppressed himself, to the death. Her heart went out with compassion to the couple at Cana. How much more was that heart, that Mother's heart, touched by the sight of the sick and the maimed and the sinful who came to her Son for solace and healing? And has her deep concern and compassion not been abundantly shown by her healing of the sinners and the sick at Lourdes and Fatima and wherever else she has appeared? Go to Lourdes and understand why we call her Health of the Sick. See not only signs of her miracles - but understand the hidden signs of her compassion for sick people who go to Lourdes sometimes much more sick than the obviously unhealthy person. Run to a mother for healing and consolation. Run to the Mother of God for deep healing and profound comfort . . .

One can imagine with what feeling she prepared the body of her son for burial along with Nicodemus - for was not Christ's blood her blood too, for his body was of her stock? But had he not given her to us as Mother too and will she not have the same compassion and care for us, her wider family? She will ask her son to cure us, or at least to give us the strength with which to bear our ills - and so we hasten to this Health of the Sick for strength and for healing. For does not the very word 'health' mean 'wholeness'? And who healthier or holier than Mary, Mother of God?

Health of the Sick, never be far from us in our weakness. Amen.

Refuge of Sinners

'O Virgin ... offer to the ear of God
The prayers of those who invoke you.
You who without corruption begot the Saviour of all,
Intercede for us, and obtain from the Lord
Joy and pardon for our sins . . .'
(pre-Seventh century)

'Refuge' is a lovely word. It denotes the safe haven from trouble, from affliction, from storm and rain, from the enemy. Those who obtain refuge or 'asylum' are saved from some sort of fate which might well have overcome them. Refuge has caused their salvation.

Salvation has caused our refuge! Christ has saved us from our sins and from the enemy, therefore he is our refuge. And his sinless Mother is surely a refuge too? To whom can we fly when we are besieged by the storms of evil and the temptation of the enemy? To the Saviour of the world who has conquered sin, and to his Mother whose heel has crushed the head of the serpent Satan.

Do not children find refuge in their mother's arms - and feel the thrill of protection when they feel the warm embrace and can mock the pursuing winds or rain or enemy?

We must learn, we sinners, that to fly temptation is often the only way out - not necessarily to stand up against it with our own puny powers. 'I cannot resist that temptation' - well, do not stand there - fly, and fly to the Mother who helped in the saving from sin and who knows well how to defeat the clever ruses of the devil.

Throughout the years thousands have flocked to her places of pilgrimage to seek her help and consolation and the mother's tender love, and to use her as a safe refuge from all harm. Under her mantle there is sure and loving protection. But first we must want to use her as asylum - we must fly to her often in the name of her Son. And this flight to the safe haven of rest under her mantle will only be a presage of our eternal haven in the presence of God, when we shall be very far from harm and where peace and light will overcome us forever. She understands our imperfections and sinfulness, and stands ready and willing to protect us - but we must make the move towards her; nor should it be hard for a son to move towards the protection of a tender and loving mother.

To Thee do I come, before Thee I stand, sinful and sorrowful:
O Mother of the Word Incarnate, despise not my petitions, but in thy clemency, hear and answer me. Amen.

Comfort of the Afflicted

'Afflicted' is a pretty strong word. It makes us think of plagues or earthquakes, serious illness or tragedy. It is a pretty strong form of trial. And there are as many forms of trial as there are people. I am sure everyone reading this will have his or her own pennyworth of affliction to contend with - and to each one, it seems the worst form possible.

And in the midst of such affliction, we wish to turn to someone to talk to about it, to tease it through, to gain an understanding of it, to see a way out - at least for a little comfort in it. Of course, we can turn to a doctor or a very good friend - but in the end, as in most trials, we are forced to turn to God, at least for explanation if not for full solution.

Who was afflicted more than Our Lord himself? He was physically afflicted and, maybe worse, mentally afflicted, and deeply hurt by ingratitude and misunderstanding and infidelity, sometimes from even his best friends. Yes, he knew what affliction was.

And after Our Lord, who better to understand sorrow and affliction than Mary, his mother? 'Mater Dolorosa' is another very fine and meaningful title for Mary - the Sorrowful Mother. Not that she spent her whole life in sadness. Who could be near Our Lord like her and remain sad for long? But there was, intentionally, great sadness in her life, for the redemption of man entailed suffering and sadness, and this sword foretold by Simeon was never far from her. Satan brought travail into the life of mankind - surely she who was to crush the head of Satan with her heel was to be immersed in this sadness, to pay, as it were, her own penalty in the anguishing act of freeing mankind from the bonds of Satan, and opening up for mankind new life, new hope, and the love of God regained.

Our own afflictions are our share in the cross of Christ - 'We make up in our own bodies what is lacking in the sufferings of Christ,' as Saint Paul boldly tells us. First, then, we must see in our own afflictions, splinters and shards of the great cross of Christ, enabling us to have a share in redemption won by him. Then we must turn to him for comfort and consolation. But if we wish better to understand woe and strife and affliction, we can turn to his mother who witnessed his suffering from close range, who had her own share of suffering, and who will fully understand our suffering. And who better than a mother to give us comfort as we fly to her? We fly, sinful and sorrowful . . . we ask her to despise not our petitions, but in her mercy to hear and answer our prayer.

Understanding ... that is surely one of her great qualities - from her own experience and from her closeness to him who suffered exquisitely and so well.

Mother of the stricken Christ, understanding and compassionate, hear our pleas for comfort in our afflictions. Amen.

Help of Christians

'O Virgin, in begetting Christ,
You have redeemed the human race.
Offer to the ear of God the prayers of those
    who invoke you.
You, who without corruption begot the Saviour of all,
intercede for us and obtain from the Lord,
joy and pardon for our sins ...
Offer your bosom to all who are created,
you who nourished the creator of all.
As a reward of service to you
extol all who come to pay their homage.
And we who are happy to serve you
will always be protected by your mediation.'
(Eighth century Book of Prayer)

The Christian is made a Christian at the moment of his baptism. Throughout his life he bears this name with pride, sharing it with his fellow Christians and delighting in the brotherhood of man under the Fatherhood of God. Alexander the Great once upbraided a young soldier, also called Alexander, for having let his name down. Could Christ upbraid you or me for letting *his* name down?

And so we turn to the great Christian, the Mother of God, for help to bear the name of her Son with pride, dignity and the fullness of love and service. We turn to her as the Mother of all Christians for example and for help. She could surely be called the greatest of all Christians, for she bore him whose name was the Anointed Saviour, Jesus Christ, and in her excellent humility, how proudly did she bear him, look after him and follow his footsteps through life to the hill of Calvary!

Being the Mother of Christ, she is, then, the mother of all Christians. Strangely and paradoxically, there may be many who call themselves Christian by token of their baptism, yet who ignore her - but she is their Mother all the same and will have her own effect on them and on their lives.

What help, then, do we who believe in her and love her, seek? Help to understand the mystery of her son, help to follow out the gospel he preached and the commands he gave, help to enter into an inner and deep relationship with him resembling her own, just help to bear his name well and to live out every moment of our lives under his banner, doing what he wishes, straining towards him who is all that matters. Let the Christian call out:

Help me, O light that brightens,
O sweetness that would divert me,
O power that would fortify me, O prop that would support me.
Remove from my lips all false and evil words,
from my mind every dismal thought.
Let your grace direct my whole life.
Mary, help of Christians, pray for me! Amen.

Queen of Angels

The final group of twelve invocations in the Litany of Loreto gives Our Lady the title QUEEN - queen of twelve groups of people. First, then, we should look at the title 'Queen'.

Christ himself is king of heaven. If we are looking for a queen in heaven, then we must turn to the concept of a Queen Mother - the Mother of Christ. That she is worthy to be called both mother and queen is quite apparent. And so, having thought a good deal about the concept of 'mother' and all the qualities this entails, we now turn to the qualities which befit a queen.

Her spouse, Joseph, the foster-father of Our Lord, was of the house and royal stock - albeit a humble part of it - of David. But, as Luke tells us, before they could come together, Mary was found to be with child through the Holy Spirit. The angel's 'full of grace' denoted not only freedom from sin and possession by God, but contained all that would go with the choice of Mary to be the mother of God. We still call a lady of charm 'graceful', and grace is really a type of charm in modern parlance. One could imagine, then, some fundamental queenly charms - courtesy and reticence, flawless manners and gentleness, delicacy and tact, modesty of demeanour and graciousness. She would be, and proved, firm in her own mind, yet docile to the mind of her master. She seemed to be a person of few words, but what she is recorded as having said was studied and meaningful. That she had great compassion and thoughtfulness towards others is magnificently illustrated at Cana. Dignity was there always, and the best of feminine characteristics.

I am more than sure she would sit easily on a throne and in her modest and humble way, even feel very much at home there, with the good of her subjects always at heart, like the great queens of every age. Indeed, the great Christian queens, of whom Margaret of Scotland is an excellent example, all had great devotion to Our Blessed Mother.

And so she who was ministered to by angels on earth has become their queen in heaven. They are the servants and messengers of God - she resembles them in this, surely, this handmaid and God-bearer. As they bowed before her on earth, it is easy to imagine their service to her in heaven, and their willingness to have her as their queen. Indeed, was not she really the greatest messenger of the Lord - thus she surpassed them in function for she brought not only messages from heaven, but the Son of God himself.

Hail, holy Queen, Mother of mercy - Hail! Our life, our sweetness and our hope . . . O clement, O loving, O sweet Virgin Mary!

Queen of Patriarchs

In the scriptures, the word 'patriarch' is used in many ways. Its more restricted use is for Abraham, Isaac and Jacob. Sometimes the concept is widened to include the twelve sons of Jacob. The name 'patriarch' is in some old writings extended to mean the heads of families, of companies of soldiers or the leaders of priestly and Levitical families.

But in all cases, whether referring to people such as Abraham and Moses, the patriarch is the leader, born so or elected, the 'father figure' of the nation or one of its tribes. In all cases, the patriarch is greatly honoured and respected by the people over whom he holds sway. His very name is revered and honoured.

That Mary should be Queen of Patriarchs means that she is the most revered amongst the revered, as it were. Certainly to the Jews and those who understand the reverence given to these father figures, to be their queen is certainly an immense honour. To be a patriarch is indeed a great honour, but to be the Queen of all Patriarchs puts Mary in a very exalted position.

They are the father figures, she is the mother figure - mother of the patriarchs, and mother of you and me. She reigns as queen over the highest leaders of all times: she reigns as queen over my heart and yours.

Another way of looking at it is this. The patriarchs throughout the ages were all endowed with gifts and qualities necessary for their important mission in life. Mary was endowed with necessary gifts too: spotlessness from the moment of her conception, calmness in her immense responsibilities, great wisdom and tenderness - above all, fullness of grace. In her unobtrusive way she was wiser than all the prophets, had all the endowments of the patriarchs: yet she bore all these not only with dignity, but with a quiet and simple poise from which we can all learn.

The patriarchs, in whatever sense we view them, stand out, as leaders do, as stars in the firmament of the world's history - gifted and capable. They are fitted by God into the jigsaw of the history of man. Mary is such a star, but of a much higher order, excelling all the others, with her unique leadership role to play in man's destiny. And so it is no wonder that patriarchs of old bow to her as she sits on her throne in heaven. Each one of them had his part to play, but they were merely preparing the ground for the unique and sublime part which Mary was to play in bringing the Messiah to reality, being the golden casket, as it were, of the Word made Flesh.

I am sure we can look on Adam as the first patriarch of all, the father of all mankind. The promise made to Adam in the garden by God, of a woman to come who would crush the serpent's head, surely links the first patriarch with the Queen of Patriarchs, Mary the Mother of God.

When you reverse the name of Adam's wife EVA, you see the AVE which was to be the first heralding of the coming of Christ through Mary.

O Mary, Queen of Patriarchs, help me realise my own tiny part in the history of mankind, and let me fulfil it well through your intercession. Amen.

Queen of Prophets

'Blessed are you, O Mary,
because in you are fulfilled the mysteries and enigmas
of the prophets.
Moses offered you in the burning bush, and in the cloud,
Jacob on the ladder which rose to heaven,
David in the Ark of the Covenant,
Ezechiel in the closed and sealed door.
Here their mysterious words are realised in your birth.
Glory to the Father who has sent his only Son,
That he should show himself through Mary,
should liberate us from sin,
and his name should be glorified in heaven and on earth.'
(Fifth century Syriac poet, Balaeus)

I suppose when most people hear the word 'prophet' they think of men or women who forecast the future. This can be true of some prophets, but the task of the prophet, chosen by God to fulfil some role in the history of the world, is much wider than that, and, indeed, more often than not the foretelling of the future does not enter his task.

The role of the prophet is simply to speak out on behalf of the Lord, often with words directly given by God, words which are not really their own. Jeremiah was amazed at being made a prophet, for he seemed to have a stammer and to be unable to speak in public - but the gift of prophecy was given him by God, and his very personal ignorance and incapability was in itself almost a gift in so far as he accepted from God what to say without the slightest possibility of his own interpretation or intervention.

I would like to think there are prophets alive today - though alas! there have always been a fair quantity of false prophets, claiming that they speak on God's behalf, but who are in actual fact only pushing themselves and duping the people with falsehoods.

It is good to think of Mary reigning in heaven as Queen of Prophets, of the great prophets of old like Samuel, Moses and Aaron, like Joel, Micah, Isaiah, Jeremiah and Ezekiel, like Nehemiah, Elijah and Elisha, and like the first New Testament Prophet, John the Baptist. It is reassuring too to think that Mary will guide the modern prophets, voices which cry in the wilderness of this life for repentance and a return to proper values, and to the worship and service of God rather than Mammon.

Yes, she will protect the gospel of her son just as she protected her son himself on earth - and will through her intercession guide today's prophets in the way of truth.

Mary, Queen of Prophets, let the truth of your Son abound. Amen.

Queen of Apostles

I suppose that after Our Lord himself, Mary's greatest admirers on earth must have been the twelve apostles. I am sure they are delighted to accept her as their queen - a heavenly continuance of their devotion to her whilst on earth. And she must have had great love for these men chosen by her son to be his closest companions on earth and the continuers of his message when he ascended to heaven. The relationship, therefore, between Mary and the twelve must have been very close, for they were the special friends and immediate helpers of her Son.

But we must not stop at that. For the word 'apostle' has a much wider connotation than the twelve apostles. Down the ages every Pope, every bishop and priest, every sister and every lay person has been in his or her own way an apostle, a continuer of the gospel, a spreader of the faith, a lover of Jesus and his mission.

The church is apostolic, dating in unbroken succession from the apostles: the bishops are special successors of the apostles, for they are leaders in apostolic works. But every Christian is born to be an apostle, to carry Christ wherever he goes or acts or works or speaks. To bring Christ out to others and in others is surely the role of each baptised person?

And the sooner each one of us realises this the better, for it opens out wide spheres of prayer and action, it brings that sense of belonging and true brotherhood, it stresses the urgency of the gospel news of salvation. And it has vast ecumenical dimensions too.

It is so very important in these days of instant communication. The apostles had no loud-hailers or amplification systems as they went from place to place, telling people of Jesus and his works and his words. As time moved on, more and more people came to populate the earth and more and more preachers were needed . . . 'How can the gospel be heard if there are no preachers . . . and how can there be preachers unless they are sent?' asks Saint Paul. 'Sent' and 'mission' are really the same words, and each one of us has an apostolic mission to fulfil in the space of his lifetime. We *are* the communicators, using every means possible. But we must have something to communicate, for we communicate ourselves first and foremost, and what the gospel has done for us and has made us.

So we are apostles and Mary is our queen. May she teach us the truth about her Son; may she introduce us more deeply to him as life goes on - and knowing him and loving him, we shall be the best communicators to our fellow men - and in this lies real apostleship!

Mary, Queen of Apostles, enrich and enlighten our poor apostolic efforts and make them fruitful. Amen.

Queen of Martyrs

The word martyr means 'witness'. Down through the ages, martyrs were unafraid to offer their very lives to witness to the fact that faith in Jesus was the besetting passion of their lives, and that they would give up life itself to defend his name and his love. 'The blood of the martyrs is the seed of the church', said John Chrysostom. It is a fact of life that the more one oppresses a good cause and makes martyrs of men and women who believe passionately in that cause, the more the cause is spread and the more life it begets.

There are many types of martyrs. There are those who literally shed their blood for the faith, like the martyrs in Rome and Japan, and even recently on the missions. There are those who suffer a more silent martyrdom - like the millions persecuted in Eastern lands. And there are those who suffer the martyrdom of sickness and handicap, and those are all around us. Nor is martyrdom restricted to physical pain - there is mental agony, the agony of being misunderstood or mistrusted, the martyrdom of being accused unjustly or not being listened to.

That Mary herself was a martyr, none could deny. She watched her son misunderstood and blasphemed, she witnessed him tried unjustly and condemned and suffering and on the cross. Hers not the literal martyrdom, but a very profound sharing in the martyrdom of the Redeemer, her Son.

And so she might well be called 'strength of martyrs', many of whom cried out for her help at that dread moment of death. And throughout the ages men and women have called to her in their various types of martyrdom. She was the witness *par excellence* to Jesus: she showed him, presented him to mankind and was willing to stand by him to the end.

Hence she is most worthy and fitting to be called the very Queen of Martyrs - proud to give their lives for their Lord. And so when each one of us has to experience a tiny martyrdom on behalf of Jesus, we cry to her for help, for explanation of our martyrdom. This makes it relevant, explicable, and thus easier to bear. For we know we are not alone, we know that our Mother shares our woes with us, and that she herself has undergone much of our suffering before us.

Let the thought of Mary, Mother of God, strengthen our resolve in fidelity to Jesus. Let us never be afraid to give open witness to our faith, no matter what the consequences, for our queen will intercede for us with her son, and we will find ourselves with a strength quite beyond ourselves. The queen is behind her subjects and will not let them down when they most need a mother and queen.

Mary, Queen of Martyrs, be with us when we are called on to suffer. Amen.

Queen of Confessors

A confessor is not just a priest to whom you go for the Sacrament of Penance. A confessor is a saint who is not a martyr. They confessed their faith in some remarkable way, if not by the shedding of their blood. Mary in the litany is named Queen of Confessors, as well as Queen of Martyrs and of Virgins.

What a variety of confessors there are in heaven! Throughout the ages these people of their time have been thrown up in history, pointing the way to their creator for a world which needed God. They are, to say the least, a varied bunch of people. Some worked on their own and contributed their own qualities to their age - not just popes and bishops and priests, but lay men and women who fearlessly upheld the gospel against all odds and gave their lives for God. Others founded groups of people to help them in their work and to continue that work down the ages, like the founders of religious orders.

We can all find amongst the saints some who appeal to us for one reason or another - it is not hard to find a patron and a friend in heaven, be it the saint after whom we are called, or whose name we took in confirmation. And of them all, Mary is queen.

Again, we must not restrict the use of 'saint' to those who are officially canonised by the church. It is a good thought to realise that surely amongst the blessed in heaven are some of our own relatives and friends who have lived loyally in the faith and have gained their eternal reward and now form part of the court of heaven.

And it makes us realise that we too are called to be saints, a term used often by Saint Paul. Maybe it is a daunting thought that you are called to sanctity too - not necessarily official designation as a saint in the church's calendar, but each one of us is called to be a saint, a unique saint fulfilling the task given us in life by God. We blush at the thought, because we use the term in a specialised way, but sanctity is the goal of each one of us. We must see that God has called us for some specific and unique task and strive, seeing it, to fulfil it.

Heaven is on the horizon, and if it seems hard to strive in stress and strain towards, then rest assured that we are not alone in the quest. We have the Lord himself on our side, we have his mother as our queen, we have the whole army of martyrs and confessors and virgins too - and this feeling of oneness with the court of heaven is indeed not only a consolation, but a vast injection of strength to our own weakness.

Mary, Queen of Confessors, help us join their ranks. Amen.

Queen of Virgins

We have already called Our Lady Holy Virgin of Virgins earlier in the litany. Now we stress that she is their queen - that, when they have triumphed and have won the crown of heaven, she is there to greet them, this Virgin of Virgins, to applaud their virginity and to welcome them to its reward forever.

The official renouncing of motherhood is most obvious in the case of nuns: women who have taken vows of poverty, obedience and chastity to release them for full and total service to Our Lord and the church. Down through the ages women have consecrated themselves to God in this way, liberating themselves, not tying themselves, by their sacred promises. They are free to have but one Lord of their lives. This does not free them from temptation, but the very making of this promise assures them of special help from God who repays generosity a hundredfold. And these commitments have enabled many of them to attain great heights of sanctity.

And there are those not officially in religious life who have taken similar vows, and though they continue to live in the world, they have pledged themselves to remain in the state of virginity for the sake of the gospel. We are blessed with many of these people in vows, in Third Orders of Religious Congregations such as the Carmelites, Dominicans and Franciscans. These are noble people who feel that though they have not the vocation to enter religious houses, they still wish to aim at a higher level of dedication in the world.

And there are those who have made this conscious decision to remain virgin, male or female, privately.

Indeed, with so much emphasis in this present world given to love in its purely sexual connotation, it is good that there are those who understand that love is a much wider concept, and that it begins with love of God and fellow men, and that only some fulfil it as married people or mothers or fathers of families. A blessing on them all - for just as fasting and penance is an expression of worship of God and renunciation of self, so virginity and the renunciation of the marital state is an expression of generosity of spirit, and is to be highly praised in those who undertake it.

So Mary is the Queen of Virgins, and to her do they turn to remain faithful to their promises to exclude physical love from their lives, to devote all love to Christ, their spouse and their Lord.

Mary, Patroness and Queen of Virgins, enable virgins to remain steadfast in their calling and divert all their love to your Son. Amen.

Queen of all Saints

'Variety is the spice of life', the old saying goes. And what a variety of saints there are - of all colours and classes and shapes and sizes, paragons of every virtue. There is no such thing as a stereotype saint. There are as many types of saint as there are people, for each one is different and reflects the glory of God in his or her own particular way. And so the lesson the saints give us is that it is within the power of all of us to become our type of saint - not falling into any particular category.

There are some virtues which all the saints have had in common. First, love of God and a deep personal relationship with God made man. Then, fidelity to the message of Christ as lived out in the particular age in history into which the saint was set. They all shared, as we do, in the 'variety of gifts' spoken of by Saint Paul, all going to make up some little replica of God's glory, so that God's glory will be manifested in all the saints in heaven - spread around his throne in harmony and perfect unity.

And Queen of them all is Mary. What we have to decide here and now is how we can fit into this glorious mosaic of goodness and love. We must look into ourselves and see how we are using our particular gifts for the glory of God and the good of our fellow men. First, we must appreciate these talents and thank God for them. Second, we must set about giving them back to God through service to his people in total generosity. For surely this was another hallmark of the saints - generosity, the total giving not of possessions and goods of this world, which count for nothing, but of their very selves, to the death. 'God wishes not your gifts, but yourself ...'

Maybe thoughts on the saints and their queen should lead us to thoughts of our own unworthiness, not just sinfulness, but ingratitude in not using the gifts with which we have been endowed, our lack of generosity. Think of the opportunities we have been given in this world, think of the daily chances we are given and all too often miss. Think of the daily blessings and favours showered on us by God. And blush to think of how we fail to appreciate them, even fail sometimes to see them. I would imagine that the most formidable part of our judgement will be the omissions, the chances missed, the graces rejected, the basic selfishness and the lack of generosity.

Let it not be so. Let us not only admire the example of the queen and the saints, but secure their active help in making us be what God wishes us to be, and has given us the power to be. Let the queen and the saints present us with the proper vision of life in general and our own lives in particular, and aid us to go forward boldly in the faith towards the goal of love, to be with the queen and the saints forever in the presence of eternal glory.

Queen of All Saints, embolden us to join the saints in heaven. Amen.

Queen Conceived Without Original Sin

Original sin was the sin of our first parents - a sin of pride, a sin of disobedience. Indeed, pride enters into all sin, for when we sin we prefer our own good to the law of God, our wills to his. Disobedience too enters into all sin, in the failure to follow the commands of God. The original rebellion against God's explicit command caused Adam and Eve to be deprived of happiness, to have to toil and sweat to master God's creation from then on.

To right this wrong demanded a supreme act of humility and obedience, an act which could be performed by God alone. And so God sent his son, Jesus Christ, to take on man's flesh, to be incarnated in all humility, a man like us in all things but sin: and to perform the greatest act of obedience possible, the giving of his own life in obedience to the will of the Father. And thus pride and disobedience were rectified by the humility and obedience of the God made man dying on the cross.

In God's process of becoming true man, he had to be born of woman; Mary was chosen from women of all time to be the mother of Jesus. No sin could touch him, for he is God. No sin could enter into his life, and thus it was necessary that his mother be free from the contamination of sin, that she herself should be totally humble and obedient. Thus,

Mary was shielded from this taint of original sin by the anticipated merits of the cross of her Son, and conceived immaculately, without trace of original sin. This was not a privilege merited by her, but by her Son; she shared his merit just as we share in it through baptism. To put it rather untheologically and simply, she was baptised before her conception, in order that the womb in which the Son of God was to be born would be completely free from sin, a spotless tabernacle, a pure shelter, an uncontaminated dwelling worthy to house the true God and true man Jesus, Saviour, Messiah promised of old.

'I am the Immaculate Conception' announced Mary as she appeared to the simple shepherd girl Bernadette at Lourdes in 1858. The poor girl could hardly pronounce the words, let alone understand them, and when she lisped them out to the authorities in Lourdes, they were confounded.

And so we call Mary 'immaculate', which word means 'free from stain', and we honour her sinlessness and utter purity. Creature though she is, she stands privileged and unique amongst mankind, and thus is the patroness of all that is pure and spotless and sinless, and the example for all to imitate.

'No impure hand can touch the one who is the living tabernacle of God!" (Ninth century)

O Mary conceived without sin, pray for us who have recourse to thee. Amen.

Queen Assumed Into Heaven

'Let us rejoice with the Mother of God,
unite in the chorus of angels and celebrate this feast
 of feasts,
the Assumption of the ever-Virgin.
On earth she was the treasure and the model of virgins,
In heaven she is as one who intercedes for all,
Favourite of God procuring for us the gifts of the Spirit,
Who with her words teaches wisdom.
The ever-Virgin Mother of God, our earth blossomed.
When she was on earth she watched o'er all;
She was like a universal providence for all the faithful.
Assumed into heaven, interceding for us,
she became a sure refuge for the human race,
near to her Son and God.' (Seventh century)

It was in the Holy Year of 1950 that Pope Pius XII solemnly defined the dogma that Mary was assumed body and soul into heaven after her death. She was not spared death, but corruption, and now reigns in heaven. This tradition of Mary's Assumption had been strong in the church from earliest times, and is in itself a logical outcome of her privilege as the chosen and immaculate Mother of God.

When or how she died is shrouded in mystery, the sort of mystery which attended much of her life on earth. But on the feast of the Assumption we celebrate the glorious day when her son took her body and soul into heaven - the spotless tabernacle which had housed him was not allowed to decay in the normal process of human corruption, was preserved spotless and immaculate and taken up forever to the glory of heaven.

We must remember that it is not just the deliberations of theologians which call out for holiness to be recognised or privilege to be acknowledged, but the faith of the people. It often happened in olden times that the holiness of a person was immediately recognised by the people of God and that the holy person was canonised almost immediately by the will of the people. The sense of God is in the people of God; their testimony concerning Our Lady throughout the ages was honoured also in the decision to announce officially this further privilege of Our Mother in being assumed into heaven.

Indeed this 'sensus fidelium', this 'sense of the faithful', is a strong element pulsing through the church. It is something intangible, but immensely powerful, as though God was voicing his will through his people - and causing them to accept or reject some or other facet of truth or falsehood.

Mary, assumed body and soul into heaven, look down on your children and bless them tenderly from your throne. Amen.

Queen of the Most Holy Rosary

There is a very beautiful picture of the martyrdom of Saint John Ogilvie at Glasgow Cross, showing the saint preparing for death, throwing a rosary into the crowd at the foot of the scaffold. The rosary, dating at least from the time of Saint Dominic (died 1221), is a really lovely rehearsal of the glories of Mary, most biblical. The Joyful Mysteries go through the key events in Mary's life: the Annunciation, the Visitation, the Birth of Jesus, the Presentation in the Temple and the Finding of the Child Jesus in the Temple. Each mystery is a wealth of thought, each well worth contemplating, each revealing new aspects on repetition. These events tell all that is to be told about the greatness of Mary. All of them are simple little stories, pregnant with meaning for man in the great tale of his redemption.

The Sorrowful Mysteries rehearse the passion and death of Jesus: the Agony in the Garden, the Scourging at the Pillar, the Crowning with Thorns, the Way of the Cross, the Crucifixion. Again, what food for thought and loving response from each one of us, becoming clearer and clearer to us the more we ponder them. And if we take the stance of Mary, looking on as these things happened to her son, the mysteries become even more startling and thrilling.

The Glorious Mysteries tell the rest of the story of Jesus, and go on to the crowning of Mary as Queen in heaven: the Resurrection, the Ascension, the Coming of the Holy Spirit on the apostles (and Mary), the Assumption of Our Lady into Heaven, and the Coronation of Mary and the glory of the saints.

The Mysteries of Light tell of Jesus' public ministry between his Baptism and his Passion. During these years of public ministry: his Baptism in the River Jordan, his self-manifestation at the wedding in Cana, his proclamation of the Kingdom of God, with his call to conversion, his Transfiguration and the Institution of the Eucharist.

All the while we ponder these great mysteries, we repeat the Hail Mary, and ply our way through the beads - a prayer of contemplation, a prayer of action, a constant repetition of Our Lady's place in salvation and her own willingness to be with us now and, especially, at the hour of our death. A simple prayer, yet one for a theologian as well as a pious servant of Mary.

How many simple folks have found all their theology in the Mass and in the Rosary! How many families have been brought up in the mysteries of the faith through this great prayer? How many men at sea, soldiers at war, people in peril have clung to these blessed beads and prayed to their Mother for help and solace? Kings and queens, saints and sinners, young and old have loved the Rosary and prayed it throughout their lives.

Of course, she is Queen of the Holy Rosary, and she must have a special love for her children who use this prayer commended throughout the ages by popes, bishops, priests and all who see the place of Mary as unique, singular and of paramount importance in their lives.

Queen of the Rosary, pray for us. Amen.

Queen of Peace

This title was added to the Litany by Pope Benedict XV during World War I. He must have looked around him in the midst of the strife and, like so many today, asked, 'What hope in this world for peace? Our hope is in Mary'.

We sometimes ask ourselves, 'Will there ever be peace in this world?' Or are war and strife a necessary part of the fallen human condition? Even today there are wars all around us, and oppression. In this welter of bloodshed and injustice, we can only turn to Mary, Queen of Peace, and invoke her aid.

Christ was born on a quiet night in the midst of peace, but he knew that his very coming would bring a sword, for men will always be divided, and powers of evil will always be around to spread dissent and disunity and strife to the point of bloodshed. And what of the future - will greater killing potential always being invented as time goes on? We can only place his world in the hands of God through Mary and never cease to strive for eventual and total peace.

But peace must start within the hearts of individuals before it can hope to spread to nations. Only a person at peace with himself can be at peace with others. Hatred of war and strife must be nurtured within each individual heart and spread outwards to families, to towns and cities and then to nations.

If you are not at peace with yourself and with your God, if you are not at peace within your own family or circle of friends, how can you hope for peace on a broader scale?

And how does peace come to a person? It comes through a deep realisation of the presence of God in the world. It comes through a profound faith that God is the author of peace. It comes from a frequent contact with God through individual and collective prayer. It comes from an understanding that the things of the earth are not for profit or gain or comfort in this world, but are given by God to be used by man in order to facilitate his progress towards Him to whom he belongs. It comes through a hatred of sin which disrupts and distorts, a hatred of greed and selfishness - it comes, like Our Lord came, in a spirit of obedience and humility. The peace which reigned over the stable in at Bethlehem was founded above all in love, love of God for us, love of man for God, epitomised in the love of a mother for her divine child.

Mary is peaceful because she sheltered Peace himself: she is peaceful because she was a mother centred in the love of her Son, which is much more important than the quarrels of nations. There can be no peace without love - and we pray to God, the author of peace, and his loving mother, for that true love which brings true peace.

Mother of God, lead us to true peace through true love. Amen.

142

Epilogue

We have now come to the end of our journey through the titles of Our Lady as contained in the old Litany of Loreto. It has been a pleasant journey, but the more one looks at these titles, the more one realises that there could be more and more to give to this tender Mother of God.

The Christian Copts of Egypt dedicated a whole month to Mary, and devote a whole liturgical book to this month, using titles such as: Virgin most Holy, City of the Great King, Church of the First-Born, Holy and Sublime Ladder, Perfect Spouse, Propitious New Heaven, Spiritual Net, and so on.

I have quoted many prayers, but there are many more. I wonder if you have ever spent time with a hymn book at the section on Our Lady, saying the words slowly and meditating on them, rather than just singing them out in church and taking them for granted? Many of them are beautiful prayers, often written by saints who throughout the ages have had immense devotion to Our Lady.

Who knows, maybe this inadequate assessment of the titles of Mary in the Litany of Loreto will spark off more curiosity, more devotion, more love of this tender Mother whom we have worshipped in the way we are permitted, creature that she was, but never really taken time to get to know better.

All could testify to the devotion of our grandparents to Mary: I wonder have we still this same devotion, and are we passing it on to future generations? We pass on so many useless and flippant trivia to young people in the way of knowledge and under the guise of education, but do we pass on the things that matter, the things that will last, the things which will stand them in good stead in times of need throughout their lives? Pass on the faith, pass on the Mass, pass on devotion to God's Mother, and you will have done your child a great service and given him much more than this world can give him, preparing him for the realities of life, death and destiny.

This lovely prayer, this litany, ends with the prayer from the Mass of Our Lady:

Grant, Lord God, that we, your servants,
may rejoice in unfailing health of mind and body,
and, through the glorious intercession of Blessed Mary
ever-Virgin,
may we be set free from present sorrow
and come to enjoy eternal happiness.
Through Christ our Lord.

Daily, daily sing to Mary, sing my soul her praises due,
All her feasts, her actions worship with the heart's devotion
true.
Lost in wondering contemplation, be her majesty confessed,
Call her Mother, call her Virgin, Happy Mother Virgin
Blessed!